D1550086

Bashevkin®
Musings for the Soul

Food for thought to inspire, uplift and hearten

Deliciously
sweetened
with the art of
Yoel Judowitz

THE POETIC WISDOM OF
CHAIM BASHEVKIN
YATED COLUMNIST AT-LARGE

BENTSH
PRESS

Bashevkin
Musings for the Soul

ISBN 0-9657697-6-3

Published by
Bentsh Press, PO Box 14, Woodmere, NY 11598
In conjunction with the Maasim Tovim Foundation

Distributed by
Feldheim Publishers
200 Airport Executive Park, Nanuet, New York 10954
(845) 356-2282

Designed and Produced by:
Dynagrafik Design Studios
125 Route 59, Monsey, New York 10952
(845) 352-1266

Cover by
TMI Torah Marketing Initiative Inc.

Illustrations
© Yoel Judowitz '10

Printed and Bound in the USA by
Noble Book Press Corp.

To order additional copies of this book
or to comment please write the publisher

The Yiddishe Momma

Like a child, he cries,
as he sways, standing there
Yet I notice, some wrinkles
And thin graying hair

And so, I approach
With a slight sense of fear
As I notice the trickles
Of tear after tear . . .

"What makes a grown man
Cry like a child?"
And ever so slightly
He beckons and smiles

"I know you are wondering,
Why a grown man would cry
Looking up toward heaven
As life passes him by

"I'll tell you, my friend
For one reason, no other
I cry like a child
As I think of my mother

"*Aishel Chayil* did Shlomo
Compose, years ago,
The essence of which
I feel, I now know

"It applies to the strength
The charm and the drama
The life and the essence
Of the '*Yiddishe* Momma'"

And then he embraced me
And his face, it did shine
"Listen, as I
Sing the praises of mine:

"The Woman of Valor
Royal, yet discreet
So many qualities
Make her complete

"Watchful, benevolent
Thrifty, content
Profound *cheshbonos*
For each effort spent

"*Gemalasa Tov V'lo Ra*
Would resonate
In all of her actions
Her manner, her gait

"*Ayin Tov*
Was her vision
Munificent, wise
Hope for the future
Through her lucid, keen eyes

"With charity, kindness
Her actions replete
From those in her home
To those from the street

"She toiled for the household fare
Her manner quiet, calm
Through tragedy of *churban*
Emunah with aplomb

"And with her husband at her side
Yibadel, L'Orech Yomim
A certain faith,
Epitomized
The words of *"Holech Tomim"*

"As candles shone
Through darkest nights
With faith, she'd check the *schoirah*
With just one mission, and one goal
To be *machzik* the Torah

"Her efforts for her family
Defy all explanation
Indeed, her toil would ensure
A future generation

"And for that generation
It is these tears, I weep
For greatness of the Momma
How will memory keep?

"I weep for
The great valor
I cry for loyalty
I sob for generations
Who won't know royalty

"Where went
The fear of heaven
Of generations past?
Where went
The toil and the sweat
Ensuring we shall last?

"Who will supply the *Hadar?*
Who will gird the *Ohz?*
Who will laugh
The *Yom Acharon*
The day God only knows

"Now you've seen the teardrops
And heard some explanations
I cry for pain that I feel now
I cry for generations"

He turned
And whispered softly
His manner strong yet mild

"A Momma is a Momma
. . . and
I'll always be her child . . . "

DEDICATED IN MEMORY OF **MRS. GENENDEL BERKOWITZ**

לע״נ מרת גינענדל בת ר׳ שלמה בערקאוויטש ע״ה

THIS VOLUME HAS LARGELY BEEN MADE POSSIBLE THROUGH THE GENEROUS SUPPORT OF
THE MAASIM TOVIM FOUNDATION

Acknowledgements

Whether it be poetry
Whether it be prose
You can't make a book
Without thanking those

Who worked with great effort
And collaborated
To bring to the market
The work I created

Above all the thanks
One goes way above
To *Avinu* in Heaven
Who guides me with love

Without His *hashgacha*
There's no if or no when
No keyboard
No fingers
No paper
No pen

No thoughts
And no musings
No time and no season
No humor
No sadness
No rhyme and
No reason

And in mortal realm
There is really no other
People to thank
Than my father and mother

They give endless guidance
And love sans condition
It's from them
If there's wisdom
In this small edition

And in the equation
They shall always figure
Thanks to the *Shver*
And his dear wife, my *Shvigger*

And after that thank you
This one, must be said
Thank you, R' Pinchos
Thank you, Yated

Thanks for allowing me
Week after week
My *kvetches*, my gripes
My musings, to speak

And thank you, Reb Yitzy,
Who stays up at night
And fixes my typos
And makes my wrongs, right

The book had an editor
Who worked hard as well
Thank you, Yehudis,
In Eretz Yisrael

I thank the designers
Who are always fantastic
Dena, Chani and Faigy
And Team Dynagrafik

The classy aesthetics
Graphic adaptations
I thank Yoel J's
Superb illustrations

The cover designers
Who came up with *shtick*
Thank you,
Yaakov Smith
And Yechiel Zlotnick

And thanks to my publisher
Who's really a *mentsh*
The fellow whose Press
Appears as a Bentsh

The printer I praise
Whose work is read global
Thank you Phil Weinreich
The printer from Noble

Of course the distributor
Who spreads prose and rhyme
My wonderful friends
At Philip Feldheim

I thank my dear namesake
Who inspired these
Dr. Michael Bashevkin
From Maimonides

Thank you for letting me
Share your good name
Your work, next to mine
Makes me seem lame

My kids, they all say
"Please don't use our name!"
I thank all their input
My thoughts, they do tame!

And to my dear sponsors
Of this publication
Thanks to you
My dear friend
And to your Foundation

Avraham Pinchus, with *mitzvos*
You're filled to the brim
Yasher Koach, Keren
Masim Tovim!
For this, and the countless
Tovos and *seforim*!

In the great harmony
Of poems and of song
A Singer, I thank
Who helped me along

A true inspiration
You always come through
For late nights of wisdom
Boruch, Thank you

But of all the thanks
That I do extend
One transcends a buddy
A pal or a friend

For this is the thanks
For my total life
Thank you, yes,
Thank you
My soul mate, my wife

May we jointly
Be *zoche*
To generations of kin
Who'll smile
And muse
About Bashevkin!

Table of Contents

On Life

Those Sacred Days

Summer

Education

Signs of the Times

Musing On Madness

A Lighter Note

In Memory

On Life

My Books

With all the advances in technology that attempt to capture one's attention, nothing is as enduring as the endless and timeless lure contained within the seforim on a bookshelf. They are there to teach, to nurture, to amuse, and to chide one into becoming a better person.

It's half past twelve
I cannot sleep
From all the rooms
Comes not a peep

I go downstairs
And make a tea
And drink
And think
So silently

In solitude
At one a.m.
Just me, alone
And all of them

Hundreds
Who can talk to me
Standing there
So silently
To guard the walls
So stealthily

They're perched
On shelves
Wall after wall
Like soldiers waiting
For the call

Each one tells
A different tale
To weave a path
An endless trail

Of thought
Of wisdom
Depth
And cheer

They stand
With me
When no one's
Here

For every mood
For each occasion
To pose a question
Or equation

To comfort me
When times are tough
When this world's words
Are not enough

They are my *seforim*
Faithful friends
That live with me
Despite the trends

3

On every topic
I could fathom
Every scene
I can imagine

No question missed
No scene is skipped
From ancient pages
Worn and ripped

Through *teshuvos*
Written
Years gone by
To *mussar*
Speaking
None too shy

The tales
Don't cease
To mesmerize
And bring
Intrigue and
Great surprise
And often tears
To fill my eyes

To brilliant *sevaros*
Lucid *psak*
Ancient Torah
Recent *hock*

My eyes
Like books
Begin to close
I look at walls of
Holy prose

And then I see
A blinking light
That beckons me
In this dark night

It shouts!
It sings!
It rants!
It raves!

With its magic
Radio waves
It beckons too
Listen to me!
I, too, can tell
A good story!

"I tell the news
I tell the tales
Of weather
Sports
And major sales

"I speak of wars
And crimes committed
Caught criminals
Who were dim-witted!"

And to my left
And to my right
My heritage
Is still in sight
What shall
Pull me
Through the night?

My friends
My teachers
They yearn to be
They'll bring out
The best in me

At arm's length
Is my destiny

It's two a.m.
I have not stirred
I have not read
Your holy word

My friends
I know
You can't at all
Help me when
You're on the wall
I know you're crying
"Play with me"

Keshaashuay
Be'onyee

Daven For Me . . .
and I'll Daven For You

Did you ever sigh
And wonder, "Why?"
About the *tzoros*
In this world?

Have you
Shaken your head
While reading Yated?
Page after page unfurled

With pleas for aid
And debts unpaid
The sick, infirm and aging
For families
In dire need
While illnesses are raging

Did you ever ponder ?
Does your mind wander
And think you just don't count?

"What can I give
So they can live
With my paltry amount?

"And though I care,
I'm no *g'vir*
I'm helpless, yes indeed
"What's done is done"
Am I someone?
To help
Those poor in need?"

Daven for Me and I'll Daven for You, is a wonderful organization that combines chessed and tefilah. People with similar needs are paired, each one davening for the other, exerting the ultimate combined power of tefilah and chessed to bring the ultimate salvation.

6

You feel you're insignificant
You sit alone, depressed
"How can I aid
A life that's frayed?
There's nothing I do best"

But deep inside
The Jewish soul
We all have a solution
With true resolve
We can involve
Our strength of elocution

It can be done, by poor or rich
It's what we all can do
A heartfelt prayer
From anywhere
To help a fellow Jew

Did you ever bear
To see a tear
That swells up in the eye
Of the older girl
Who's such a pearl
Yet hasn't found her guy?

"But I'm no *shadchan*
I know no one
How can I help their plight?"
Don't you believe?
Can't you perceive?
To say
Tehillim each night?

We often sit
With palms turned up
"There's nothing I can do"
When we see pain
We think we're plain
Forget that we are who

Yes! We are the ones
We can relieve
The sadness that we see
The prayers of each
And every Jew
Can change eternity

"I have no lights nor sirens
I'm not part of *Chaveirim*
I have no team
Sometimes I seem
Alone, as if in *chairem*"

But my friend
You're not alone
Through *tefilah*
We're connected
You simply cannot disengage
Your *tefilos* are expected

"I was never honored
At a dinner
No speeches for me, said
I'm your average
Chaim Yankel
No pictures in Yated"

"I have no cards
For clergy
Stuck in my billfold
I have no
Special access pass
I go where I am told

"I haven't learned
'bout CPR
Or Heimlich's maneuver
I'm just an average quiet *Yid*
No shaker and no mover"

Oh no! My friend
I must amend
Your simple point of view
If you think that's reality
You haven't got a clue

The power of the cure
Comes not from checks alone
But from the tears
And from the prayers
That reached the holy throne

There are so many of us
Who may, too, be in need
And if a partnership, we form
Hashem will intercede

You often sit alone yourself
Mired in despair
How would it be
If you and me
Would, that one *tzorah* share?

To know that somewhere
In this world
You have some special friends
Who *daven* every day for you
So that your sadness ends

And while those *tefilos*
Shatter walls
Your world's no longer grim
For as your friend
Davens for you
You pray for her or him

The greatest *chessed*
We can do
And help ourselves as well
Is worrying for others
Salvation to compel

And as you bear the burden
Your friend will bear it, too
So please, my friend,
Daven for me
    ... and I'll *daven* for you

The Metal Box

$\mathcal{A}$ metal box
Suspended from
Wires in a tower
The minutes that
They wait for it
Seem often like an hour

They stand outside
The cubicle
They know not where it is
And somehow up
And down the chute
The cubicle does whiz

They stand around
In waiting
Some smile
And some frown
Some wait for it
To take them up
Some wait
To take them down

And soon more people gather
The buttons they keep pressing
Will the "up" or "down" come first
Everybody's guessing

And then there's always someone
Who does not trust the light
He'll push that button once again
And he will push it right

Visiting hospitals and office buildings, Bashevkin noticed how divergent worlds converge and compact into one tiny location. And in that small place, all cultures and backgrounds are basically forsaken. For all of them, the focus is usually upon one objective. And no matter how different they may be outside the box, inside, they are very much the same.

And then another
Comes along
"Your push does not suffice.
You only pushed it one more time
But I will push it twice!"

And finally that metal box
Gently it does stop
And opens up its doors to those
Who'd like to reach the top

Some once-cramped
Now shuffle out
While others shuffle in
The man who wants
To go down, waits
The "up ones," look and grin

And now the box is filled again
Each person holds his place
Each one's careful
Not to stare
At anybody's face

The button ritual resumes
But now there's
So much more
For fifteen people
Want to push
The button for their floor

"Can you please press
The number four"
"Oh! I need number seven"
"I'm getting off on the next floor"
"Can you please press eleven?"

Each one has his place to go
Each his destination
And when they're crammed
Inside that box
They all have the sensation

They're moving up
They're moving down
The box does rise and fall
They think they're going places
But they go
             . . . nowhere at all

They grunt and smile sheepishly
And talk about the weather
They're locked out
From the outside world
They're all in this together

Suspended by a cable
Hanging in mid air
Above the ground
Hundreds of feet
Not going anywhere

And in the back
Of each one's mind
Are thoughts
Perhaps they think
Subconsciously
They speculate
"What if
This box
Would sink?"

For just the stop of power
Can bind their lives forever
As their whole fate
Does bear the weight
Of some gears and a lever

They cannot use their cell phones
Blackberry's no reception
They all must face each other
With truth and no deception

They stare at the certificate
To check if it is Otis®
An accidental human sound
They take pains not to notice

Indeed inside that box they live
The moments they're together
And somehow
Different lives are bound
By the box held by a tether

And when the bell chimes
At their stops
They go their merry way
Not ever thinking back upon
That moment in their day

When strangers stood
Inside a box
Suspended by a tether
That tied the world
Of different folk
For moments, all together

11

The Bagel Shop

plain w/side	2 55	eggs w/fries
Tuna special	4 75	smoked fish
plain w/ salad	6 50	veg/ soup
white fish	4 50	muffins
cream cheese	3 00	garlic knots
plain w/ butter	1 50	coffe/tea

THANK

Did you ever think
The choice you have
In each aspect of living?
And I mean not
In what to learn
Or what charity you're giving

I went into
The bagel store
Just the other day
The counter was
Immaculate
Behind it an array

Of bagels of all sorts
Of types
And flavors forms and sizes
Varieties
I never knew
Some plain and some surprises

*Standing in line
at a bagel café,
Bashevkin watches
people of all sorts.
Some of them spit
out orders in the
staccato clarity
of a machine
gun, while others
think about their
decision as if it
would be a life
altering moment
that will define
their future.*

It came my turn
And I did learn
That nothing is quite *poshut*
"Mister," they said
"Please order now!
And if you can, please rush it!"

I looked around
Quite hurriedly
At all the spreads and cheeses
They were not nice
They pushed me twice
There were no "Thanks" nor
"Pleases"

"I'll take a bagel"
I just said
"Perhaps a bit of fish"
They looked at me
Quite quizzically
"Excuse me, what's your wish?

"What type of bagel
Do you want
Onion, pepper, plain?
Jalapeños, cinnamon?"
The man would not refrain!

But I stopped his
Soliloquy
"Onion would be fine"
Behind me, there was muttering
Coming from the line

"Would you like
That toasted
Perhaps we scoop it out?
The fish you asked
To put on it
Tuna fish or trout?

"Or maybe you want lox
My friend,
Smoked or even sable
Whatever your desire
In this store
We are able!"

I can go on, my friend,
And tell you
'Bout the mayo
And drinks they had
Like cappuccino
And some crème de cacao

"Do you want
The fat free spread?
Perhaps a shmear of butter?"

"Hurry" they hissed
Their turn they missed!
Once again
They'd mutter

"We have three types
Of tuna fish
And fancy albacore . . ."

I really did not
Want to hear
I wanted
Out the door!

But others
Well behind me
Reveled with their voices
Debating about
Poppy seeds
And all the other choices

The point I thought
That here in life
We have so much to choose
And life is good
So think we should
"How can we ever lose?"

Such wonderful
Selections of
Charity and learning

Indeed, my friend,
It does not end
But we must have
A yearning

To choose the
Proper delicacy
To satiate
The soul

And that's
More of
A holy choice
Than an onion, poppy roll

Why people spend their time
To think
With or without seeds
And hardly give a passing though
To those with special needs

For that great
Restaurant of Life
Offers a great menu
And you can choose
Delicacies
No matter what the venue

And if I had a choice to choose
And a song of good to sing
The bagel that I'd surely choose
Is called the "everything"

For those choices are silly
Yet some care what they choose.
Spend time
On choices
Serious
That way you'll never lose …

The Meshulach

Sometimes at a Simcha, we make snide remarks or subtle denigrations of the collectors, those poor souls who come around to solicit funds for their families. But how many of us try to relate to their plight, with the appreciation that with but for a twist of fate, our roles could have, Heaven forbid, be possibly switched?

I sat there at the *Simcha*
Shmoozing with my friends
Sipping on the finest scotch
The *chevra* recommends

We'd talk about
The latest news
How mortgage rates
Would tank

And how to get
The greatest deal from
That troubled
Texas bank

The eight-piece band
Was playing loud
And festive
Was the mood

As the fellows
Sipped their
Glenlivet
While masticating food

And then he came
A-calling
A paper in his hand
The misery
Deep in his eyes
Cried louder than the band

He shuffled toward our table
And no one seemed to look
We were engrossed
Another toast!
And notice, no one took

He stood there, mute
His life reduced
To the paper
In his hand
With signatures
From rabbis of
This strange and
Foreign land

The crumpled paper
Told a tale
Of misery and woe
Of illness, debt
And bills unpaid
That none of us
Did know

"Why do they not
Look up at me?
What have I done to them?
What is it on this paper that
They all seem to condemn?

"I too have a family
A life I feel is rich
Of learning in the holy Mir
For no *gelt* I would switch

"Aren't I
The sole supporter
A *Rebbe*,
Husband,
Father?

"But to the guys
All sipping schnapps
I'm nothing but
A bother"

He stared at me
As if to say
"Am I different than you?
Am I less important than
Your Johnnie Walker Blue?

"Did I not sit
Across the way
When you learned in
The Mir?
And answered
All your questions
And made
The *sugya* clear

"I'd explain
Reb Nochum's words
With dignity and honor
And never mock
The struggles of
The 'Green *Americana*'

"And when the dorm
Was really cold
And the cholent
Was cold too
You'd pop into
My humble home
We'd set a place
For you

"You bummed a
Cigarette off me
When you ran
Out of Time®
I never asked
From you one back
Not once a single dime

"And now my life
Has been reduced
To stories on this page
You just look
For a signature
And look not at a sage"

And suddenly
My eye does see
A vague, familiar face
Some decades back
Like centuries
Another time and place

"Is it him?
Oh! Can it be?"
I thought
Behind my drink.
"Can he be
The *Yungermahn*
Who taught me
How to think?

Is he the one
Who always came
Each freezing
Thursday night
And sent hot kugel
To my dorm
To everyone's delight?

Is he the one
Who had ten kids
By now, perhaps
It's more

But never
To another soul
Would he ever
Close the door?"

I banged upon the table
And everybody turned
To listen to
The lesson that
I suddenly
Had learned

"We oft reduce our
Fellow man
To papers he presents
And think how much
That sheet is worth
In just dollars and cents

"But oft beneath
The plastic sheet
That holds
The approbation
Is one great soul
That played a role
Beyond evaluation"

And so, my friend
The next time
The *shnorrer*
Comes around
The drinks will stop
Let chatter cease
The band won't make a sound

I won't look at the paper
What it says
I do not care
The man who holds
That sheet once held

My hand

. . . Back in the Mir

Dead Man Talking

I listen to a *Daf Yomi* shiur
When I get into my car
I don't cover much ground each day
I don't drive very far

But a few weeks ago
A voice stirred me
As I heard the words he said
It hit me like a thunderbolt

          . . . The *Magid Shiur* was dead

I know these words
Do sound quite rash
Not polished nor refined

But learning from
A dead man's voice
It really scared my mind

I mean, I learn *Gemara,*
And other *seforim,* too
I know that all the great one's "live"
That's what *Chazal* tell you

But, I really knew the man
His face
In front of me
I hear the *shiur* and and tremble as
I hear his *Daf Yomi*

The proliferation of Torah tapes, now from so many sages and Talmidei Chachomim who are no longer with us, left me with a haunted feeling and new meaning to the Talmudic adage that the lips of the righteous move in the grave when their Torah is taught.

Bashevkin wrote this after listening to a Daf Yomi Shiur from the great gaon, Rav Yitzchok Isbee, whose wonderful shiurim are recorded by Dial-A-Daf.

19

I stopped and thought a moment
I shut the sound and cried
I understood that one can teach
Long after he has died

Can I, too, leave a legacy
Where all my work is new
And passed from generations
From old to youngest Jew

I try to live this life for now
But longer I shall strive
That what I do in this "dead world"
Will forever stay alive

*L*ast week I asked
A boy I met
If he knew a certain name
'Twas not a politician
Or an athlete of great fame

It was the name
Of someone
One person or another
It was the name
Of a young man
It ended *"ben* a mother"

"Would you know
Someone named Gilad?
His mother's name's Aviva"

"I don't think I have heard of him
Is he in our *yeshiva*?

"In this Yeshiva
We don't call
The boys by mother's names
So if you want some info
Don't play those silly games

His mom could be Aviva
Or Sarah or Irit
Without his last name
I am sure
I can't help you a bit"

We daven for so many people and for so many things, but often we forget that one or two moments a day can do so much for those who do not even know of you. Yet your tefilos are so meaningful to them.

21

Alas, the fellow
Did not know
Gilad is nowhere near
Alas, he would
Have known the name
If he would, really care

I asked another young man
About his locked-up brother
"Would you know Yaakov Yosef
and Raizel is his mother?"
"I have no idea
Just who he is
Ask me about another!"

"Have you heard of
Yoel Zev ben Mirel Risa Chava?"
He shuffled in the coffee room
And took a sip of java

"There is a man in Butler
His name's Yehonaton"

"Why should I know
Why did he go?
Was it something he'd done?"

"Yosef ben Yitta Rivka
Does that name ring a bell?
While you're out on the avenue
He's sitting in a cell

"Shalom Mordechai ben Rivka
Is his name on your list?
For all the good he's done for you
In *tzarah* is he missed?

"A *yid* named Sholom Mordecha
Whose plight united those
Whose diverse worlds
Indeed converged
In prayers they'd juxtapose

"A name that so inspired
An entire world to pray
For Tinok ben Aviva
Tehillim did you say?

Indeed, there are so many
The souls who need our prayers
Can you imagine what it means
Knowing someone cares?

I know that it is hard to stop
From daily mundane chores
To cry for someone else's pain
To bang on Heaven's doors

But don't we shake a *lulav*
Proclaim, "All Jews are one!"
How do we live that message
When *Simchas Torah's* done?

Can we find it in our heart
To let someone's pain in?
And a huge door
We'll open for
Redemption to begin

Their tears will
Mingle with our cries
And flood the Heaven's gate
And soon enough
The pain will end
And so will our wait

For all of us have
Why to cry
And pain we do endure
But we can ease
Our selfish cries
If we would add some more

And all the tears
We shed in prayer
Will form a great big sea
Tears from here and there
Will flow
From them and you and me

Indeed a mighty ocean
With waves that rise and roar
Will sweep the pain
And misery
Of pestilence and war
And on the waves
Will ride the folk
Whose cries
Had formed its surge
As Master of
Redemption's ship
Will suddenly emerge

And in the wake will follow
The tears of joy and glee
For we will ride *geulah*'s wave
To our home and destiny

The Tie

I will not lie
I don't know why
This musing is
About a tie

Not a tie
Like in a race
Not a tie
Like a shoelace

I know a tie
Is quite mundane
Perhaps, I should
And will, explain

This tie, I wear,
Means much to me
I got it as a
Gift, you see
And on its back says
"Brioni"

This tie it goes
Around my neck
They say it costs
A hefty check

I would not know
I'd never pay
But I just love
When people say
"What a nice tie
You have today!"

I don't know what
My gifter spent
Or what the gift
Did represent
But when I go
To an event
I wear the gift
That he had sent

I save it for
A special day
A *bar mitzvah*
A *Yom Tov* day
And then I fold
And put away
This gift I got
The other day

I wore it to a *bris*
I wore it to a wedding
I loved the hordes
Of compliments
I seemed to
Keep on getting

Yes compliments!
I wanted more
I walked into
A fancy store

Bashevkin received a gift that he appreciated more than he thought he would. It was a Brioni tie. The fellow who gifted it chided Bashevkin to cherish it and take care of it as it cost more than his suit. Bashevkin thought he would not be impressed. But as he wore the tie, he began to appreciate it more and more and learned a bit about life in addition to a few sartorial lessons as well. Thus an ode to ...

I sauntered to
The fashion guy
And asked him
"Do you like my tie?"

"Oh! Yes! I do
I must admit"
And then he looked
Again at it

"It's really nice"
He said to me
He knew it was
A Brioni

But then again
He looked at me
His eyes in shock
Filled with pity

"You have to buy
A suit to match
Dispose your old suit
With the patch"

"It's beautiful
But here's to boot
Your tie, it costs
More than your suit!

And then he added
In a huff
"You need a shirt
With a French cuff"

"You cannot wear
A Brioni
When your suit
Is half poly!"

A pair of cufflinks
He soon sold
"Nothing less
Than solid gold"

And now my
Credit card's maxed out
With stuff that I once
Did without

But there the story
Does not end
There's one speck more,
My engaged friend

You ask of me
A speck? A speck?
Well, now I am
A total wreck!

I tell you this
I don't know why
That speck it landed
On my tie

And I say this
With so much pain
I really could not
Clean the stain

And you can't have
Some cherry pie
Stain your new
Brioni tie

And so the point
Is now quite moot
What shall I do
With my new suit

My shirt with cuffs
The man had sold
The cufflinks made
From solid gold?

My tie is stained
I have to go
Bu there's a point
That you should know

That sometimes
What is wearable
Can also be
A parable

A City On High

Shavuos in Lakewood, New Jersey, where thousands sit and learn day and night, evoked many emotions. Bashevkin remembers Lakewood during the days of Rav Shneur Kotler, when the community was basically confined to about one square mile and two or three enclaves of apartments. Today, there are scores of communities spread across miles and miles of land with new developments reaching miles from the center point of 617 6th Street. It is a heartwarming testimony to the growth of Torah through the accomplishments of Bais Medrash Govoha.

I closed my eyes for 50 years
And as a world went by
From ashes smoldering on the ground
A city rose on high

All I saw were forests
And dirt roads lined with trees
As old men on park benches
Would share a summer's breeze

The forest grew for flowers
And trees were there for wood
I saw not the potential world
The world that said, "We could"

The farms they were aplenty
Hotels around the lake
A sleeping giant's slumber would
Somehow soon awake

As no one saw the *shtenders*
That would come from the bark
They did not see the fire
Ignited from the spark

I could not see in autumn's wind
The forest leaves that swayed
Would one day be pages
From whence the thousands prayed

And people looked at forests
And saw a branch, a limb
And in this town, beside the lake
Those woods are now *seforim*

For they only saw dirt roads
Places no one could live
They saw old men
Who would all die
They had nothing to give

They saw a rabbi who would cry
"*Torah lishmah*," he'd rail
They laughed and thought,
"How out-of-date!
Of course his dream would fail!"

I woke up from my slumber
And everywhere I went
Families came streaming
From the Torah's newfound tent

Park Avenue and Village Park
The Villas and West Gate
Hearthstone, Regency, White Oa
Lakeview and The Estate

From Coventry to Chateau Park
And way down Fourteenth Stree
They *tumul* of a world thought lo
By those who did retreat

The children play in Brookhill
There's Torah in Red Oak
The *Rashba* thrives in Pine River
PRV for older folk

They learn all hours in the night
Continue on all day
Returning to their holy homes
In Negbah and Agway

28

And everywhere
The skeptics laughed
Homes filled up with *seforim*
And every block is building new
Mikva'os, *shuls*, *chadorim*

And children walking
In the streets
Thousands to each *cheder*
Skipping to *Bais Yaakovs*
And rushing to a *seder*

From Kedmah and
Queen's Gardens
Torah, *avodah* there
Chesed in Lakewood Commons
And in Louisburg Square

And hundreds of *minyanim*
And *gemachs* for "just in case"
In Arlington and Wyndam
Of course in Sterling Place

Shiurim every hour
In person and on air
From Private Way to Elmwood
And to Washington Square

Where once were only trees
And forests damp and dark
The spark ignited, lit the world
In Sterling, Forest Park

And everywhere I go
I see the dream
Of *yungeleit* fulfilled
A Torah ocean overflowed
To outskirts it has spilled

New England Village
Prospect Park
The Pines are Whispering
And Raintree, Spruce
A Street called High
Together they all sing

From Chestnut, Presidential
Central Avenue
From Clifton's ancient bakeries
Since 1942

The cars line up so quietly
A mission so Divine
That starts from halls of BMG
To way down County Line

From homes on Ridge
And Kennedy
To Sunset, corner James
They share the aspirations
The hopes, the dreams, the aims

Whether it is Hope Chapel
Or down to Miller Road
A spirit that defies this world
In each humble abode

Has *golus* seen
This revival
New Central Avenue?
Where thousands learn
And some do earn
Enough to get them through

Yes, Central Avenue was old
And now there's one that's New
Make no mistake
Around the Lake
They're building Torah, too

Each Forest now a neighborhood
Let us not forget
That woods that once just held
Birds and trees
Are Woods of Somerset

Humbly the *aishes chayil*
With patience, sits and waits
He'll sit and learn
And then return
To Primavera Estates

The "Pines" that
Once held Laurels
And hotels' fancy suites
Are bustling with *Yiddishkeit*
On Pine Groves and Pine Streets

Who thought
That this could happen
When times were bleak and dark
Who thought a home of Torah
Would thrive in Central Park?

For from a tiny building
Filled with blood, sweat and tears
Arose a shining city
In sixty-some-odd years

The seeds, with love, were planted
Some sixty years ago
On land, watered with purity
All they would do was grow

And so *kanfei nesharim*
Will have so much to bear
To carry all the Torah homes
From Route Nine through the air

And in the center of the crowd
We'll all come out to meet
The Mother of these holy homes
617 6th Street

For from a simple, humble house
On Sixth and Private Way
Arose a kingdom of Torah
We celebrate today

A day like any other
As children went to *cheder*
A humble part of Williamsburg
A broken elevator

The elevator's empty shaft
Forever filled with tears
A scene of Divine destiny
A parent's greatest fears

Headlines in the New York news
On the radio it played
A very private tragedy
Publicly displayed

Then I thought perhaps this *tzara*
Was made for us to hear
And show another type of *Yid*
Indeed, we all do care

And so I drove across the bridge
To the tears of Clymer Street
I thought I would be different
Than anyone I'd meet

They'd look at me, they'd stare
Why did this man come?
A relative? A reporter?
Where is he really from?

In August of 2008, Yaakov Neuman, a 5-year-old boy, fell down an elevator shaft after the elevator became stuck on the 11th floor of the Taylor-Wythe Houses at 70 Clymer Street in Williamsburg. Shiva in apartment 11-B was attended by Jews from all stripes and persuasions. This is a story of an encounter at the Shiva home on Clymer Street.

I'd see a room of red-eyed men
All dressed in Satmar black
I'd sit, then say *"HaMakom"*
And leave and not come back

And so I walked down
Clymer Street
Through cops and news abound
I shuffled toward the entrance
My eyes locked on the ground

I walked into the building
And all that I did see
Were different sorts of *Yidden*
All for 11-B

One had a *kippah s'rugah,*
A polo-shirted Jew
A blind young man
Who thought to come
A *talmid* of YU

We all walked in together
The warmth — it filled the air
The solace of the *achdus*
Helped dry a father's tear

And no one looked in disbelief
For simply through the day
Jews of every stripe and color
Came all just to say . . .

That we are here to join you
In this, the saddest pain
Until *techias hameisim*
Until *Moshiach's* reign

I left the room quite moved
As I downed eleven flights
And realized why our nation
Can reach the highest heights

As I left the building
A man was entering
We both were not *Chassidish*
We both thought the same thing

He wore a sporty polo shirt
He drove a fancy car
A Sephardic Jew, I figured
His name, it was "Amar"

I don't know why I did it
I asked him why he came
He looked at me in wonder
And I deserve the blame

The answer he said, "Simple."
In a voice so calm and mild
"This *tzara* is not just for one
He's *Klal Yisroel's* child"

The news I know they blasted it
Through every single borough
For them it was sensation
For us, collective sorrow

To join our worlds together
Despite the way we look
For *Yidden* to hold hands
   once more
A tragedy it took

But now I know we're closer
As Yaakov's *neshama* soars
For we have forged together
Behind those broken doors

And though we may look
   quite different
One day we will meet
Holding hands together
In joy on Clymer Street

Shattered Summer

It comes a time, too often
When summer's skies turn gray
And thunder shakes the heavens
And night engulfs the day

And all our dreams of sunny days
Are shattered by the sound
Of children's hopes
And parents dreams
Crashing to the ground

The robust breaths of childhood
Choked by a speeding ball
The Torah of a child stilled
By an elevator fall

A young girl's smiles crushed
Plunged down a hole, destroyed
A speeding truck
In seconds struck
To leave such dreadful void

And strewn about the shattered lives
As generations weep
A broken nation wakes once more
From apathetic sleep

And tears, they fill up streams of pain
In bedrock once thought dry
Indeed they'd fill an ocean vast
Each teardrop asking, "Why?"

It seems that tragically every summer Klal Yisrael is beset by calamity. Accidents, drownings, and illness shatter the calm of vacation time, reminding us that until Moshiach comes, there is no respite from sorrow, even during the carefree summer months. This was written in memory of a three-year-old boy who was tragically hit by a truck in front of his bungalow colony, in the summer of 2009, and for all the tragic losses of children through the year.

Why
Does the sun stop shining?
Does laughter turn to tears?
Does healthy life turn sickly?
Do children sleep with fears?

Why
Do the rockets fall on us?
Do monsters hate us so?
Do some of us turn on our own?
I fear, I'll never know

And yet the hope lies in our faith
Of one great Master Plan
On the rivers that were hewed
From tears of mortal man

A ship shall carry calming news
Across their silent wake
That all the tears that formed their mass
Were only a mistake

For one day skies shall sparkle
As little children play
And never will we cry again
As sun shines on our day

And grass will dance
And trees will sway
And mountains will soon sing
When all the pain
He will explain,
Our kind and gracious King

"Wow! See the trees!
They're beautiful"
He said that summer day
Indeed the sun
Was shining bright
As he left the house to play

And each tree
It stood there proud
Its leaves so green and bright
But something
Did intrigue him
About that pretty sight

"Yes, the leaves
Are beautiful
Oh what a pretty scene
But somehow it gets boring
'Cause all the leaves are green!"

And then the skies
They darkened
And the sun did not shine bright
And summer's sunshine
Seemed to pass
And switched to autumn's night

And once again
He went to play
With hardly any sun
When times were
Tough and cloudy
And there was not much fun

Sometimes our differences are more pronounced and prejudice prevails, but if we think wisely we will all realize that in the deep essence of our existence, we are all one.

And as he looked up
At the leaves
Not one of them the same
The young boy
Looked concerned
As he plodded through his game

Each leaf this time
Was different
Some yellow, brown and red
No longer were
They uniform
The differences widespread

And so the boy
Philosophized
'Bout summer, leaves and green
He said some words
That stuck with me
With insight, pure and keen

"I guess when things
Are sunny
And all is in full bloom
We think that all
Is just the same
Assumptions, we presume

But when the clouds
Are on the scene
And winter's breath is bleak
Each leaf assumes
Distinction
And each one is unique

And I stare at
Each one's differences
And the beauty of each shade
I see it in the
Dark of fall
Its artistry displayed

Sometimes sunshine
Blurs the lines
Like leaves we're just a scene
A blur of sunny branches
A giant clump of green

But when the pall
Of a dark fall
Casts shadows on our greens
Our colors show
And we then know
We each bear special genes

Recession Proof

The recession of 2008 surely gave pause to all of us to ponder and muse about the items and investments in life that are truly recession-proof.

𝒜 year ago
I was riding high
On the salary they paid
I traded up
My old Accord
And bought an Escalade

My stocks were soaring
To the sky
Investing was a cinch
Just pick the banks
WaMu, Citi
And then call
Merrill Lynch

They said to buy
Some real estate
A condo somewhere h[...]
Of course
I was conservative
(I did not buy a yacht!)

Needed cash
For my big world
My friend, it was real ea[...]
"Just sign this form"
My banker said
Then smiled
Oh! How sleazy

38

I took the cash
And bought more stock
And then some real estate

I tried to buy
In Florida
But "I came in too late"

I took my cash
And flung it round
On every single journey
I begged my friends
Who flew with me
"Please, get me into
    Bernie"

I rushed to make
All sorts of deals
I had money to burn
"Dear kids," I said
"I'm busy now
I have no time to learn"

I saw that they
Were saddened
One even shed a tear
So I took off
Some time for them
An hour here and there

Of course I gave
Some *tzedaka*
They gave me a nice plaque
I said
"I just don't need it"
But they wouldn't take it back

I thought that it
Was too fancy
With letters etched in gold
I stuck it somewhere
In a box
With stuff dusty and old

"I cannot hang this
On my wall!
Kavod is not for me"
The *Rosh Yeshiva* smiled
As he eyed my SUV

And then that week
In *Elul*
When everything did crash
And suddenly
No SUV

No stocks,
No bonds,
No cash

My condo
It was worthless
Who needed one of those?
My banker was still smiling
When he said
That he'd foreclose

Who was there
To help me?
Who could I turn to?
The door was locked
At Lehman
And bolted at WaMu

I had to dump
The Escalade
For a beat up Chevrolet
I tried to sell
My fancy house
For a price no one would pay

I realized I had nothing
My wealth
Was but a dream
Somehow Upstairs
They showed me that
We're not smart, as we seem

I no longer sit on *mizrach*
And no one seeks advice
Can't buy *Atah Hareisah*
I just can't pay the price

But what I really
Do have left
That they can't take from me
Is all that I invested
In my eternity

And then it really hit me
One thing I would not lack
The donation to the *yeshiva*
And that dusty, gold-etched
plaque

And the moments
I spent with the kids
And the time I gave to learn
Will stay with me
Much longer than
The money I did earn

So during this recession
One investment please do make
The time and *gelt* you give for Go
No one can ever take

The Crisis Crisis

𝓜y muse this week
Won't be the nicest
As I explore
A word call "Crisis"

When I first heard it
The world did bristle
Remember a "Crisis"
Of Cuban Missile?

Look it up
In your history book
What to be called
A "crisis" took

A world was perched
With great alarm
About to drop an
Atom bomb

Now that's a crisis
I would say
'Cause a nuclear bomb
Could spoil your day

But now that word
Yes, quite absurd,
Applies to
Every problem heard

Yes, homework's tough
And mortgages fell
And we wait to hear
A wedding bell

But a word once used
For nuclear war
Is now applied
Like never before

And crisis is not
Alone abused
Holocaust
Is way, too used

Of course, I worry
About the poor
And attacks
Around Darfur

But no matter how bad
No matter what's lost
How dare you call it
"Holocaust"

The numbers there
Will outlast time
That magnitude
Of heinous crime

It seems that everything is called crisis or disaster these days. Perhaps we are taking difficulties to the extreme and forgetting what the meaning of a true crisis really is.

And yet the pols
Who politic
Everywhere
That term they stick
It's enough to make one sick

One other phrase
That ticks me off
"I'm 'very sick'
I have a cough"

Don't ever use
That word or two
Even if
You got the flu

"Very sick"
A scary term
If used for colds
It makes me squirm

When patients often
I did see
Dripping chemo
From IV

So dare not be
So brash and bold
To use 'very sick'
For a common cold

(Unless of course
You're 82
And then you come down
With the flu)

So let's tone down
Our hyped-up use
Of words
That suffer from abuse

And put discomfort
Even pain
In right perspective
Once again

Disaster is
Another word
Whose overuse
Is quite absurd

I mean a cleaners
Made a stain
Okay, perhaps
That is a pain

But disaster?
Give me a break
It's a stain, my friend
Not an earthquake!

Your mustard shmear
Dripped from salami
It's a stain,
Not a tsunami!

Did you ever say
"This is the *worst*
How terrible!
I must be cursed"

When something happens
That causes fears
Just think back
'bout 60 years

Before you say
"This is the *worst*"
Step back
And think
About it first

So when things
Are tough
And you feel sick
Cool it
On the rhetoric

And use some words
That are reflective
Of a life that's put
In true perspective

Forget Me Not

*Gedolei Yisrael
are constantly
beseeched to help
others in need.
But when they
plea to us to help
others, do we
really take heed?
The story of Yosef,
languishing in
prison, forsaken
by the Sar
HaMashkim,
whom he helped,
is reminiscent of
many of the times
we foresake those
who advised us
and guided us to
good fortune.*

*F*or two long years
He languished there
'Cause the one he trusted
Well, he just didn't care

Yes, Yosef
Had helped him
Interpret a dream
But helping him get out
The man didn't deem

It wasn't from hatred
And not even from malice
The fellow was busy
Pouring wine in a palace

He may have
Thought about him
The kid who was in jail
"I remember that he helped me
But forget the detail"

"Of course, I am grateful
I'll send him a check
But right now, I'm busy
It's a pain in the neck…"

So Yosef did languish
While the *Sar* poured the booze
'Til the day he'd take credit
With nothing to lose

"I can't help him now
I'll get to him soon
At a time and a place
That I find opportune"

I flip through the pages
Of every paper
I think I pull
That very caper

The pages are filled
With names that I know
They ask for assistance
They have nowhere to go

Reb Chaim, Rav Shteinman
Rav Michel Yehudah
They're asking and pleading
The Badatz and Agudah

They plea for our *tzaros*
For they really care
Do we give
When they ask
For *Kupat Ha'ir*?

Or do we say
"Sometime
Later
Next year"?

Rav Shmuel, Rav Aharon
Chachomim all *shlit"a*
They ask and they all sign
For *Keren HaShmittah*

And we all know
It's important
And we all plan to give
But they "languish in prison"
While the good life, we live

Each day with their Torah
They interpret "our dreams"
But I think we forget them
Or, so it seems

And we pour drinks at *simchos*
And we're all *Sar Hamashkim*
While we simply forget
The holy *Misaskim*

They say, "Please remember
We now are in need"
But do we forget them?
Their cries do we heed?

And when there's an ad
From a languishing sage
Do I say, "I'll soon help"
And then turn the page?

Do we scream
And we shout
'Bout Eretz Yisrael
But for Yerushalayim
"Oh what" and "Oh well..."?

"It's *Shabbos*! It's *Yom Tov*!
I'll give to them later"
And the ads are then fed
To the incinerator?

We smile of course
And say, "We'll remember"
But wake up, *rabbosai*
It's already December!

It's not that we're cheap
Or that our values are skewed
It's just that we're busy
As a butler or steward

So when you read
The paper
Take note of the pages
The pleas of *Gedolim*
The world's greatest sages

And respond
With some gusto
With no reservation
"I should help this *tzedaka*
And give a donation
I asked *them* to *daven*
When I needed salvation"

Now it's time to remember
When they ask
"Yes!" I'll say
"I won't do it tomorrow
I'll do it today"

Once Upon a Niggun

Do you remember days of yore
We kept watch through the night
We sang and "watched the eagles soar"
And the words they fit just right

The drums they banged much slower
Guitars no juice, just string
And "Time to Say Good *Shabbos*"
Was a song that they would sing

It seemed "like no tomorrow"
When they sang slow, not fast
Of "hopes for our future"
And "dreams of our past"

Dr. Middos "taught the way we lived"
And Shnookie liked to hide
Boruch learned his *brachos*
There was Zaidy's Old East Side

We saw it "in the clouds above"
And "in an echo's roar"
We sang the songs of Hashem's love
"Ten thousand times before"

Maybe my hair is turning grey
And it has been a while
We sang the songs of "Zaidy"
And an "old man's gentle smile"

The world of music has surely changed in the 40 years since the Rabbi's Sons produced their first album. Bashevkin muses about the good old days when music was soft, the words were clear and the tenor was understandable.

47

We sang of *Sifrei Torah*
Saved but sold for money
We saw "Hashem in sorrow
Keili - lamah azavtani"

We sang of "blind and shallow"
And of the "web of sin"
We sang of "hallowed rooms'
And "tears amidst the din"

I think the words we sang
Made sense
And some were even fun
Who can deny that up on High
"Hashem, Yisroel and Torah
 . . . are One"

We "threw away our hammers"
We had "nothing left to do"
And Nikolai behind the wall
Wanted to be a Jew

There are songs
I thought were fast
Some I thought were slow
But time has passed
So speedily
The new songs I don't know

Our Father up in Heaven
He watched from High Above
As we *shuckled* slowly
While we sang
And "turned to Him for love"

Nazis burst in midst the songs
Their "plight it pierced my soul
Today those tearful *niggunim*
Are replaced with rock and roll

But kids still sway in earnest
Although their beat is loud
And I can't make
The moves they do
Or dance with that fast crowd

But each *dor* has its way to sing
And they all come from the heart
And I think that I can harmonize
Though we're many years apart

No matter what the *niggun*
With *heartz* I sure am certain
Soon "great walls of the *Heichal*
Will replace the Iron Curtain"

Nothing to Say

Sometimes a situation is so sad or so intense that putting it into prose and, more so, putting it into poetry, diminishes the unwritten magnitude that it deserves. Bashevkin tells the story of a visit to Memorial Sloan Kettering Hospital on York and 70th in Manhattan and the impact it had on his outlook won life.

I sat down at my desk
Last Wednesday night
Thinking of
What next to write

Of course there's always
What to say
On any topic
Any day

Thursday came,
I had to go
What would I write?
I did not know

And on my way
Into the city
What can I write
What would I say
I'm sure I'll know
By the end of the day

There was someone
I had to see
Not far from York
And Seventy

But then he called me
On my phone
"The meeting," he said
"I must postpone."

And thus I stood there
Across from Sloan
On York and 70
Alone

Perhaps I'd take in
A strange sight
Which would give me
What to write

Perhaps I'd muse and
Put that in
A scene from streets of
Manhattan

But I remembered
A dear friend
Who said, "Each week
That time I spend

"To help a child
On Thursdays
Who gets chemo
And gamma rays"

So I decided to stop by
Be *mechazek*, just say,
"Hi!"

49

Then I'd go back
Cross the street
To see the man
I meant to meet

I took the elevator
To the ninth floor
What would I find
Behind the door?
The quiet emptiness
Of a hospital ward?
A lonely face
Someone who's bored?

Perhaps a nurse
Or two?
Or three?
A child tethered
To IV?

My friends, I write
I can't forget
What my eyes saw
Soon made them wet

Not one, not two, not even three
It was almost like a large city
Chassidim, Misnagdim
I just could not count
I could not fathom the amount

Yiddishe Kinder
Rachmana litzlan
My heart did cry
For every one

Some worn down
By heavy weight
Told what to anticipate
Others' eyes
Filled with the void
Of lives disrupted,
Hopes destroyed

Every spot taken
No empty spaces
Just empty looks
On cherubic faces

Corners, cubicles
Separated by drapes
IVs in
All sizes and shapes

Children missing all their hair
Mothers filled with thoughts
   and fear
Tehillim said some here and there
To the only One
Who could repair
The damage that
I saw in there

Of course there were some
Rays of light
Who brought some hope
To darkest night
To those with redness
In their eyes
Chai Lifeline brought some
Pizza pies
A smile brought to one so sick
By a *chossid* doing magic *shtick*

But nothing dulled the shock
I saw
On Sloan-Kettering's
Pediatric floor

Never in my imagination
To see a place
Like Central Station
Filled with such
Yiddishe pain
In my mind
Always remain

I returned home with
My mind numb
To apathy
Would I succumb?

And before I got a chance
To ask
Life sent me
On a simple task

Mundane
Of course
I had to run
And go and buy
A staple gun

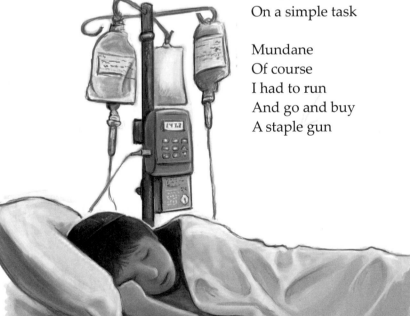

I went inside the hardware store
A lady was looking at a door
I think a knob was what
   she needed
She looked quite smug
Perhaps conceited

"Mister?" she chimed
"Crystal or Steel?
Which will have
The best appeal?

"Could you get gold?
Would that be hard?
They'll hold me
In such high regard

"But maybe copper
Is good enough
It looks real nice
And handles tough

"On second thought
Gold plate is nice"
She looked at me
Did not think twice

"You look quite smart
Are you a Jew?
There is something
I must ask you

"I'm standing in
This hardware store
Almost an hour
Maybe more
Thinking of the perfect door
Is this my life?
There must be more!

"Why can't I decide
What knob to buy?
Is there a *Jewish*
Reason why?

"Why do I care?
Why do I vie?
About what type of
Knob to buy?

"Is something
Really wrong with me?
If I value
The most petty?

"I know I look like some
Rich snob
Wasting time
On a door knob"

"Lady," I said
"I think I'm sure
About the knobs
For your front door

"I do not mean
To disrespect
But there is something
That I suspect"

I thought and spoke
With no great ease,
"It's all about
Priorities

"I thought about
That dreaded floor
I thought about
Your silly door

"I will not mock you
Nor deride
The reason
That you can't decide

"I know why
I sure can tell
'Cause everyone
At home
Is well!"

She looked at me
And sadly nodded
About the point
I gently prodded

Perhaps it takes
A trip to Sloan
To value
Things that are our own

And not waste our time
On petty things
While pain lives on
In Kettering

I will not write
'Bout Berry-blacks
Or Crocs or robes
Or Kipling sacks

Today I think 'bout kids on nine
And pray that they
Will all be fine
And if we focus on what matters
And skip a week of silly chatters

They'll come home soon
All feeling well
And then next week
I guess I'll spell

My thoughts on
Other mundane stuff
But not this week
It's just
Too tough

Name Game

During the Bernie
Madoff scandal,
the name Ponzi
scheme came up.
Bashevkin was
interested in how
that name came to
be and what other
institutions have
taken the names of
heroes or villains.
Learning that the
name Ponzi scheme
was coined after
the chicanery of
Charles Ponzi, he
investigated and
wrote these lines.

*A*midst the troubles
Of the times
I took a break
From silly rhymes

To look at words
How things are named
How they become
The things we blamed

What's a Ponzi?
Would you think
A guy named Charlie
Made a stink

He took from Peter
To pay Paul
And on he went
Until his fall!

Ponzi's name
So it would seem
Forever linked
With that bad scheme

But he may now
Lose all the blame
Now that
Madoff did the same

Okay, Ponzi
Did it first
But Bernie *oy*
Was he the worst!

But names can also
Stay for good
America is
One that should

Amerigo Vespucci
He came to
Before Chris came
In '92

A name forever
Linked with "mean"
Is that of Dr.
Guillotine

He meant for good
The ax was dull
His way was easy
On the skull
Well, his intent
Was void and null

Because he's known
For the worst time
They'd send you there
For any crime

A lynch is something
Considered vile
Convict and hang
Without a trial

It came from
Judge William Lynch
Who found himself
Quite in a pinch

Too many crimes
Not enough courts
He said capture and punish
For all sorts!

There are some names
That light a lamp
André Marié Ampére
Got the name "Amp"

I know that may not
Mean a lot
Especially if
Your name is Watt!

If you don't like science
Here's what's new
If food is something
That's for you
You might thank
An "Earl"
Named Montague

He was an "Earl"
Which meant quite rich
He "earled" in a town
Called Sandwich!

He liked to slap
Two breads on meat
The Earl of Sandwich
Made that treat

You don't say
"Give me
Shmeared bread"
You ask for a
Sandwich, instead!

Gets too hot
Or cold at night?
Celsius
And Fahrenheit!

They're the guys
Who measured heat
They make
Thermometers complete

Names we make
Can rise, can sink
Next time we act
We ought to think

Like good oil
Great names do rise
It's all one has
The day he dies

Lekach Tov

*T*he numbers do not
Bode too well
The nation's in recession
And if it's me
That feels the hurt
I guess it's called
Depression

And *kollelim*
Are filling up
With those without employ
To find a place
Of *ruchniyus*
To fill their lives with joy
To join those
Who toil hard
For in Torah is their joy

And from the busy
Trading desk
Or other forms of labor
The fellow
From Wall Street
Has just become his neighbor

They sit and
"*Kvetch the benk*"
With one thing on their minds
That no matter
How high one has climbed
The *Aibishter* reminds

During a recession, no material possessions are guaranteed. The only item guaranteed is the knowledge of Torah that one retains. It is a priceless possession that does not get lost, no matter what the turbulent times may bring.

That He is in
Total control
Parnassah is at will
For poor or rich
No matter which
He controls the till

And those who mocked
The *kollel* man
With mismatched doors
On cars
And laughed at him
While drinking *shnapps*
And smoking fat cigars

Now come to realize
That they too
Are sticking out their hand
And realize now
That nothing goes
Exactly as they planned

Chazal tell us
A story
About a long boat ride
The passengers
Were wealthy men
Who showed a sense of pride

They brought their wares
Upon the ship
To sell them 'cross the sea
Each one had
A shipment worth
A very hefty fee

But there was one
Lone traveler
Who had not brought a trunk
He had no packages with him
No goods
No gifts
No junk

The wealthy men
They mocked him
"What do you have to sell?
Who needs your type
Of merchandise?
When we make out so well?"

He was a
Talmid chochom
And all he had was "trust"
Which came to use
Quite handily
At the wind's first gust

For a storm it went
A ragin'
And the waves they shook
  the ship
And bags and trunks
Went overboard
As winds began to whip

And when the sea
Subsided
And no one had their wares
The *talmid chochom*
Smiled
As if he had no cares

"Ki lekach tov nosati"
My *sechorah* I still kept
While all the goods
You thought you owned
Into the sea were swept

My friends
A storm is raging
And stuff's been lost at sea
But find the time
Amidst the storm
To buy eternity

No matter
What they do to you
Whatever scam they try
The *lekach tov*
You get today
Will be your greatest buy

The Apostrophe

All too often I see signs that read "CD's For Sale" or the 70's and expressions like "a Torah and it's crown." I often wonder who those 70s belonged to? And cringe when I decontract the words to read "A Sefer Torah and it is crown." And though I am no "Strunk and White," the improper use of apostrophes irked Bashevkin enough to jot a few lines about it.

*A*postrophe
A tiny line
It can make
Possessions mine

And that is good
It's very fine
But it's not always
So benign

It can make
Two words as one
Now that can be
A lot of fun

Should have
Could have
To Could've
Should've
And definitely
I surely
Would've

But it's too often
Used with ease
These funny
Apostrophes

Like the guy
Who sold CD's
(Right after the 70's)

Are parent's called
To come to school?
Whoops! I think someone
Just broke a rule

Unless of course
The parent's kid
Something
Very wrong he did

But not as bad
You will agree
As misusing
An apostrophe

Of course the time
It's most misused
Its placement
Is indeed confused

Is when they miss
The word "it is"
And think that it's
Meaning his

Or take a phrase
"The girl's like spaghetti"
(Now I do not mean
To get petty)

59

But if you mean
That she is thin
The apostrophe
It does stay in

(You do not have
To be a wiz
To know that it
Contracts "girl is")

But if it's noodles
She enjoys
(Girls like spaghetti
So do boys)

Then it means
That girls love oodles
Of that special
Treat of noodles

And then, of course,
No little line
For "Girls like"
Is really fine

There are some uses
And some other's
Like a bunch of
Mother's mothers

(Does others
Get apostrophe?
If mothers do
Belong to me?)

A sign was printed
Large and grand
"WE'RE HERE TO HELP
TO LEND A HAND"
They want to help
You understand

But if the apostrophe
Was not put on
They were here to help
But now they're gone!

And now you know
About a dash
The rules I don't
Want to rehash

Just realize
A little line
Can change a word
Or just combine

And if a little line
That could
Think about the power of…
Kutzo shel Yud

Life's A Book

THE STORY OF REB YOU

Over the last twenty years more and more Torah biographies, and anecdotal books have touched thousands of Jewish souls. Imagine if we lived our lives as if we would all be published?

*A*t times
At me
I take
A look
And wish
My life
Was worth
A book

To live
My life
So perfectly
A true
Torah
Biography

I surely know
That, that's
Not me
But …

If I could act
Differently
They'd write stories
Extolling me

The way
I think
The path
I took
Imagine
I'd be
A whole book!

A whole book
Written
Just for me
A new *gadol*
Biography

And all my life
Would be on stage
With words of
Wisdom
On each page

He never said
A silly joke
Nor as a teen
Did take a smoke
And never
Lashon horah spoke
Would not react
If they'd provoke
From insults
He did look away
He wished them all
A pleasant day

If doors would slam
Upon his hand
He would not scream
He'd understand

Support one widow
Maybe more
And slip large checks
Under her door

If I could be
A *maggid's* tale
Where each *nisayon*
I'd prevail

And live the life of
Mussar talks
And speak the speaks
And walk the walks

I'd run to open
Every door
Help the homeless
Sick and poor

I'd be "A *Tzaddik*
In Your Times"
Whose life is sung
With tunes and rhymes

My *Divrei* Torah
Each week said
My picture plastered
In Yated

My picture hung
In Jewish homes
And featured
In Bashevkin poems

(And there again
My *gaavah* roams)

The crowds
Would pass
And shake
My hand
And jump
At every
Small command

That life you think
Is awfully grand
To live in
A fantasy land...

My friend,
You do not understand

For each of us
Does have a book

Each day
The One Above
Does look
At every step
We ever took

That book
Is read
By only One
Whose review
Has just begun

For every year
We are on stage
Our lives do shout
From each
Great page

A book we wrote
Of our own choosing
More *chashuv* than
Bashevkin's Musing

Indeed we write
The book
That counts
In which
Is detailed
Every ounce

No wishes
We have
Of grandeur
For in that book
We're all obscure

And when
He reads
And writes
The *p'sak*
We stand and cry
And bang
And knock

Beseech, bemoan
Request, implore
Begging Him
"Open the Door"
Please let me write
A little more

And in that book's
Great paginations
There are no bluffs,
Exaggerations
No fantasies,
Imaginations

And thus the chapters
We shall write
Every moment
Day and night

Start today
For all our days

A chance
We have
To mend
Our ways

For He cares not
Up in the skies
Of Books and blogs
Or latest *Neis*

And every second
We are using
Counts not
Towards articles
Or musing

For what is written
In His book
Is all
He'll see

That's where
He'll look

And so I'll
End this
Little rhyme
And work
On poems
That outlast time

And are
Inscribed
Eternally
In Books
Hashem
Will always see

Ain Od Milvado

*I*s summer really winter?
Except for cold and snows
Is "The Country" just the city?
Except for grass and bungalows?

Is swimming really walking?
Except that you're in a pool
Is Davening just talking?
Except that you're in shul?

Do you daven at the Kosel
Or just talk to a wall?
Do you see the holiness you wish for
Or see nothing at all?

Is learning only reading
But the language of the book?
Is eating only breathing
Just you chew the air you took?

Is crying really laughing?
Except from whence the tears
Is sadness really happiness
If you'd allay the fears?

Are you really learning something
If you just go to school?
Is one you think is brilliant
Just another fool?

Are articles inspiring?
Is advice written, sage?
Or are the words you read today
Just there to fill a page?

Existentialism is a difficult topic that I know not much about. But often I have to stop and realize that the whole world and all of nature is only a manifestation of the Almighty.

Does one soap get you cleaner?
Or is the world just hype
Do I just pontificate
As I sit here and type?

Do you see only darkness
While others see just light?
Do you somehow
See the harmony
While others see the fight?

Do you really give *tzedaka*
Or just plain "pay your dues"?
Do you react to pain and hurt
With truth, or just a ruse?

Are you acting in sincerity?
Is your smile just a frown
When you are standing
On your head
And smile upside down?

Rabbi Akiva laughs
When all his friends do cry
Some, perhaps will say,
"Why not?"
When others ask
Just, "Why?"

I wonder if the worlds diverse
One day will really sync
Will there ever come a time
When all the world will think

There is no summer, winter
There is no rain or snow
There is no city, country
Nowhere to run or go

And all my strange
    philosophies
They do not mean a thing
And all the tunes I try to hum
Don't mean that I can sing

There is no happy
And no sad
There is no east and west

There is no bad
There is no good
There is no worst or best

There are no places
Left to see
There's no fun stuff to do

The only thing that I do know
That I'm a *Yid*, A Jew

And yes, indeed,
There is one thing
That makes me think it so
Because this world does
Not exist
Except
        . . . *Ain Od Milvado*

Nowhere to Hide

*T*hey say a man can surely run
But lo, he cannot hide,
I'd like to share a story that
Shook me up inside

Johanna Ganthaler
Who hailed from Italy
Embarked upon a journey
Far across the sea

She traveled to Brazil
With her husband, pensioner,
And then they'd "tour de France"
And travel through the air

And so, the two were slated
To travel on Air France
The flight was four forty seven
And that was not by chance

For that plane, it went missing
Somewhere in the sea
And yes, she should have boarded it
Back to Italy

And many people thought, indeed,
She met her destiny
Pitiful as all of those
Lost somewhere in the sea

But no, it did not happen
As the lady missed the flight

In June of 2009, an Italian woman who arrived late for an Air France plane flight that subsequently crashed into the Atlantic, was killed in a car accident a week later. Some may say fate works in mysterious ways. Bashevkin guesses that when it is one's time to go, even if the Malach HaMaves takes a detour, he still gets to his mark.

67

And what was consternation
Now seemed quite all right

She lived to tell her story
Of how death she had cheated
The *Malach Hamaves* had lost
And he went home defeated

I guess she felt real good
And surely thanked the Lord
That unlike all the others
She was not on board

They took a plane from Rio
And traveled on their way
And spent some time in Austria
On a sunny springtime day

But she forgot a lesson
Which all of us should know
That *din* will follow you around
Wherever you may go

And so she and her husband
To Austria they went
But the *Malach*'s reaching hand
She could not circumvent

For on the road in Kufstein
There was no lady luck
And the woman who had
Missed her flight
Crashed into a truck!

And so thus ends the saga
A lesson we should know
That when you're on the hit list
There's nowhere you can go

Each bullet has an address
Each bomb a place to blow
And without *siyata dishmaya*
There's nowhere safe to go

All's Well

*T*his story, my friends
Is really old
It started by the well
It continues to this very day
As everyone does tell

The *tefilos* are no different
"Please help me find my mate"
Some call it a *p'gisha*
And others say "a date"

But look at Rivka's *yichus*
Don't look so very *"teef"*
Her father was a scoundrel
Her brother was a thief

They just wanted the money
From rich Avraham's slave
The food they served
Was tainted
Is that how to behave?

But 'Laizer looked right past that
He looked not at a *shver*
In fact only one *shailah*
Did Eliezer *kler*

The water rushed to Rivka
But he was not impressed
He did not look for miracles
He had another test

The term "shidduch crisis" has become part of the Yeshiva vernacular. If we would follow the path of the Avos in looking for a mate, perhaps we would not have a crisis at all.

69

Will she say, "Can I help you?
Perhaps you need a drink
Your camels look quite thirsty
They also need, I think"

And somehow that's what
Clinched it
That's what saw it through
And now B'suel's Rivka
Is Rivka *Imainu*.

It was not her great *yichus*
Or bags she filled with dough
That brought the cloud
To Sora's tent
Or made the *nairos* glow

So stop and think
Young *yungerman*
When deciding what to do
If it worked for Yitzchok
Can it also work for you?

Indeed our *Avos*
Not like us
Married fast
Without a fuss

One sent a servant
One fine day
Stood by a well
To hope and pray

That Miss Right
Would come his way
Draw the water
And then say

"Mister
Would you like to drink?"
That was all
To forge the link

No resumé
No *shtick*
No stink
Can we do it?
I don't think

He did not ask
He did not care
What type of shoes
Or size she'd wear

Just the one
Who'd come on by
And offer drinks
In full supply

What does her brother
Really do?
He did not ask
No interview

Where for high school?
Where for sem?
Questions like that
None of them

Do they cook
Or take-out food
Does Mom wear *shaitel?*
Tichel? Snood?

Does she have big
Or real small feet?
Do they ever
Serve chopped meat?

Soup from scratch?
Do they use broth?
Plastic, linen tablecloth?

Paper plates
Or fancy china?
Plastic dishes?
That's a *tayna?*

Leizer, Yaakov
Had no sheet
Prerequisites
Before the meet

At least one issue
Was foregone
No girls from
That place Cana'an

Lucky for us
Lucky for them
The land of Canaan
Had no sem!

I hope
I did not
Touch a nerve
But perhaps
Our girls
They do deserve
A chance to meet
Based on their soul
Two who share
A common goal

And if we rid
The silly issues
And tears
Would dry
And no more tissues

One crisis
Would at least
Be done . . .

. . . And then
We'll find
Another one

Give Me the Strength

I beg for the capacity
To hear the daily sorrow
The ill, the poor
Thrown out their door
Who fear for their
   tomorrow

Of captured soldiers
In our land
The boy hit by a missile
The poor boys locked up
In Japan
My skin, my soul does
   bristle

The neighbor
Newly diagnosed
The child plagued
With cancer
The teen who almost
Overdosed
The questions
With no answer

I ask Hashem
"Give me the heart
So I can bear the pain
And pray each day
And do my part
Not nod and blurt
  'Amein'"

The capacity
To cry and weep
Yet somehow
Live with joy
To share my strength
With those quite meek
With fear of no employ

To show the world
With confidence
And ease
The consternation
Of those whose lives
Hang doubtfully
By strings
Of desperation

To have enough
Emunah
So others glean
The strength
To walk them through
Their tough terrain
No matter what
The length

I think of the *gedolim*
Whose homes
Have been a haven
For unknown told
Who bared their souls
With faces etched
   and graven

The lines of people's
Misery
Stretch far beyond their faces
Yet somehow solace
They do find
In those homes and holy places

Their hearts they have
Oh! So much room
So much capacity
As they sit
With superhuman strength
And warm tenacity

Give me the heart
To hear the cries
Yet somehow not get down
To hear the pain
And then to make
A smile from a frown

Give me the strength
To hear the grief
And somehow find solutions
To share the pain
Yet ease it, too
With my small
    contributions

If we let them
Lean upon
Our loving, caring shoulder
Our lives will have
A warmer feel
When all is growing colder

We all do have it
In us
Despite our weary world
And soon we'll see
Our destiny
His banner raised, unfurled

73

All in A Day's Work

*I*t was after the Yomim Tovim
That I began to muse
As life went back to normal
For all my fellow Jews

The *sukkah's* down
The *s'chach* is packed
And winter's chill is felt
In fact a bit depressed we feel
When routine we are dealt

And after *Pesach,* dishes packed
And countertops are gone
Hagados packed away with them
With wine stains still left on

As all of us trudge back to work
Benafsho yovi lachmo
With the curse *"bezei'as apecha"*
Five thousand years ago

Adam le'ameil yulad
No matter what his *facht*
We *shvitz* and plan
To make a buck
Yosheiv in *himmel lacht*

And some manage
To bring home bread
And others pile bills
While some attempt
To ply a trade
And others hone their skills

After the long Yomim Tovim of Sukkos and Pesach, we all trudge back to our mundane work. Last year, a few weeks after a long Yom Tov vacation, Bashevkin visited a Yeshiva late at night. There he saw Kollel fellows, some already grandfathers, who had been there all day learning They were still literally sweating in the toil of Torah. It gave Bashevkin a new perspective on work.

The secretaries
Type their work
While bosses scream for more
And clerics sleep
At cluttered desks
And *kvetch* that life's a bore

And laborers
Will now return
To mix mortar and bricks
And carpenters
Will pack their belts
With tools that help them fix

The bell will ring
And they'll go home
To lead another life
Some return to parents
Others to a wife

And some will kiss
Their *kinderlach*
Forget about their work
And mumble stuff
About their boss
And how he goes berserk

But then there are some others
Who never leave their trade
They work all day
And much of night
And little they are paid

Some may think it's easy
Perhaps they've not been there
To see the sweat of *ameilus*
In Lakewood, Brisk and Mir

I know you may be skeptical
You work from nine to five
And think you have the hardest job
Of any man alive

But try, my friend, an hour
To leave your *"daf* and *shiur"*
Prepare a deep *chaburah*
For thirty men to hear

Explain why a *Nesivos*
Or even a *Ketzos*
Who say a *p'shat*
That it is not
A *stirah* to *Tosfos*

Prepare a *shiur* in *Eiruvin*
Define a *Telzer klehr*
Try sitting seven hours straight
Over Reb Boruch Ber

Adam le'ameil yulad
No matter what his *facht*
But lucky is the man who sweats
In Torah just to *tracht*

Those Sacred Days

Shabbos Shtiklach

*M*onn did not fall
On *Shabbos* day
For yesterday's was
Put away

A double portion
Yom Shishi
Lechem Mishneh
Actually

Double fell
The day before
Not because
We needed more

I walked into a restaurant in Brooklyn on a weekday night and saw all the Shabbos delicacies being served and devoured by a group of pious looking men. I was troubled – can't they wait until Shabbos? On the flip side many recent inventions have been designed to, I would venture to say, circumnavigate the many restrictions of Shabbos, Bashevkin decided to hearken back to the Good Old Days when things were simpler and more basic. Without making weekdays into Shabbos or Shabbos into weekdays…

But *Shabbos*
It just
Would not
Arrive
On Friday's twice
We would all thrive

And that would be
The *Shabbos* treat
Chulent or *kugel*
Salty, sweet

Somehow *Shabbos*
Was unique
The day that people
Reached their peak

A culmination
Of the week
With different acts
And different speak

Special foods
Just for that day
Klal Yisroel
Put away

Now I think
How times have changed
Our menus are now
Rearranged

To make the week
Part *Shabbosdik*
Is it real
Or is it *shtick*?

Kugel made
Was for that day
A special dish
Just put away
When Totty came
From where he'd pray

But now *kugel*'s
A different venue
A "special" on
The deli's menu

Okay
I hear
It tastes so good
And *Yidden* are always
In the mood
For a taste
Of *Shabbos* food!

Now I'm not petty
Nor will quibble
If on Friday
We just nibble

But let's
Save something
Let's hold back
Keep one dish
A *Shabbos* snack

And there's another
Shabbos dish
Appears with *kugel*
And with fish

It seems that no one
Just can wait
They serve it early
Serve it late

Is it strange?
Am I insane
Upset that *chulent*'s
Now mundane?
But *Shabbos* too
Has lost its charm
A *Shabbos* clock
With an alarm

A *Shabbos* light
A special box
A *shtick* to go
With *Shabbos* clocks

Newfangled lamps
To read in bed
Shabbos cream
To make lips red

Now I hear that
There's a rush
To make a kosher
Shabbos brush

And, oh,
My friends,
Please have no fear
It's for your teeth
Not for your hair
(That's been around
At least a year!)

So weekdays now have
Shabbos food
And *Shabbos* day
A weekday mood

With clocks
And timers
Toothpaste, too

All for the
Observant Jew

81

Make-up
Peelers
Water heaters
Crock pots
Timers
Bells
And chimers

Don't get me wrong
They all are fun
But I just think
About the *monn*

It fell just Friday
And
Forget it
There was no other
Way to get it

A whole People
A whole Nation
Did not need
An innovation

I'm not sure now
What I would do
Without my
Shabbos Shticklach too

But we have found
A way
Around
With inventions
Quite profound!

Sometimes I long
In many ways
For *shtick-less*
Invention-less
Good ol' days

Wake Up Call

The alarm clock starts to ring
At first I think I'm dreaming
After all, my sleep is deep
And the sound is hardly screaming

But it blares despite my sleep
To wake me from my slumber
But thirty days is far away
To me it's just a number…

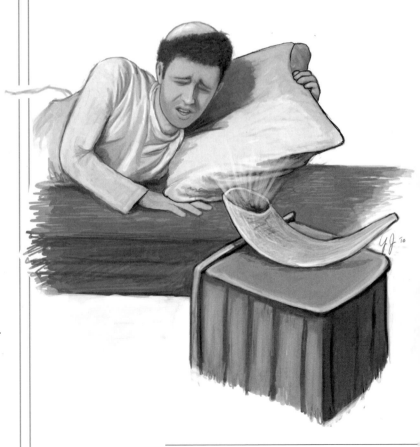

*The constant call
of the Shofar
during Elul is like
the alarm clock
of teshuvah. We
must not push the
snooze button!*

That same alarm
It blasts each day
Its constancy should shake me
I try to sleep
The sound is deep
The blast meant to awake me

For as the calendar
Nears the day
That I, indeed, must rise
That piercing sound
The King is crowned
Open up your eyes!

For on that day
The sound shall say
Today's the day they reckon
And hear the cry
You can't deny
To you they call and beckon

Awake! Awake!
With cries and blasts
Arise now from your daze!
There is no button
Labeled "snooze"
It's time to mend your ways

Again, again
The whole month long
Those shofar blasts
Should wake you
For every day
You sleep away
And nothing seems
To shake you

Then just think back
A year gone by
With tears and so much harm
And that, my friend,
We must all mend
Wake up to the alarm!

What does it take
For us to wake
From sleep that's apathetic
Invigorate
Before that date
And become energetic

That on the day of
Reckoning
Triumphant blasts shall sound
To pave the way
For that great day
When we are homeward bound

Summer of Elul

$\mathcal{A}$nd as the summer
Swelters on
And children keep on playing
In other worlds
Just south of them
Their elders are now praying

For as the horns
Of ice cream trucks
Still play that boring tune
Another horn
Does blast each day
To say what's coming soon

The calendar
Can play real tricks
And lead us to forget
That sun and sand
Will not prevent
The day to pay our debt

And though the days
Of *Elul* come
While bungalows are teeming
And kids are splashing
Up in camps
And summer sun is steaming

Sometimes the calendar plays tricks on us and the secular summer season carries on almost until Rosh HaShana. We may be frolicking in the sunshine, but the Yom HaDin is quietly approaching.

The mighty court
In Heaven
Has now opened its books
And down upon
His creatures
The Holy One He looks

So though we may
Be stuck somewhere
Away from *Elul* mode
Perhaps somewhere
Where summer reigns
In a tiny, hot abode

There are still
Opportunities
To rise to the occasion
Even though you
Told your boss
That "I'm still on vacation"

For *chesed*
Opportunities
And those of *limud Torah*
They need not an
Official *shul*
A *rebbi* or a *morah*

No matter where
You all may be
In camp, away, at home
The calendar
It speaks clearer
Than this Bashevkin poem

For as you pack
Your suitcases
To bring home Labor Day
The *Yom Hadin*
Will soon begin
In just another day

So all this writer
Says to you
As you bask in the sun
Please don't forget
There is time yet
Yemei Harachamim's begun!

The Doctor

The doctor's office
Cloaked in dread
A somber spirit
Looms

Uneasiness
Uncertainty
Fills each one
Of the rooms

The tears are clearly
Palpable
The husband
And the wife
Is there anything
That we can do
That may just
Save his life

"I'm sorry,"
Said the doctor
"There's nothing
I can do
I wish there was
Some miracle
That I could offer you."

Dejected
They both
Left the room
Depressed and
All alone

When suddenly
A ring was heard
Coming from
The phone

The doctor
Found a protocol!
He said it's guaranteed!
And so the couple
Rushed back in
With superhuman speed

"It may take
Too much effort"
The doctor did explain
"And nausea
And tiredness
And often
Bouts of pain"

Of course! Of course!
We'll all comply
If this shall
bring the cure!

No Task
You ask
Is beyond us
We're positive!
We're sure!

*We are given
a prescription
for teshuva. Do
we follow it as
meticulously as the
prescriptions given
for the common
illnesses we suffer?*

We'll wake up
Before dawn each day
We'll follow protocol!
We'll listen to
Each word you say
We'll miss nothing at all

We'll read instructions
Carefully
We will not skip a word
We would not skip
A thing you say
For that would be absurd!

We'll watch our actions
Cautiously
We'll eat what you prescribed
We'll study what
The Doctor said
With every word transcribed

Yes! Somehow when
We think "it works"
No treatment
Is a pain

We follow
Every therapy
With zest
And won't complain

Imagine that the Doctor
Who truly holds the key
Would tell us the prescription
To true eternity

We'd wake up hours
Before dawn
And read
Each *slicha*
Slowly
We'd open up
Our eyes and ears
To only items holy

We'd follow
Shaarei Teshuva
Like a sacred
Guide to cure
If we believed
In every word
If we were really sure

Would it be hard?
To learn some more
And give more charity?
Recite each *bracha*
Loud and clear
And *bentsh* with clarity?

If we'd believe
The Doctor said
That this
Would work for sure
We'd follow
Every protocol
Not treat it like a chore!

We're in the Elul Hospital
The prognosis
Is grim
They said that there
May not be hope
To save our life and limb

And suddenly
Almighty
The Doctor
Gave the cure
Prescribed it
And He promised us
Recovery for sure

But suddenly
We're tired
We'd like to
Fall asleep

Not listen
When the
Shofar sounds
And not wake up
And weep

If only
The Almighty
Would wear
A nice white coat
And come in
With a stethoscope
On every word
We'd dote

So wake up
My dear readers
Let's follow the
Prescription
And I'm sure
Health and happiness
Will be
Our great inscription

What I Hear

I stand by my seat quietly
The echoes filled with awe
And though I heard the sounds
So many times before

The varied thoughts that fill my head
Arise in symphony
Behold a new year heralded
With all its majesty

And each time that I hear a blast
Another thought does rise
They dance in perfect harmony
Before my tear-filled eyes

The *shofar* sounds declaring
His Majesty is King
Of all of His creation
Human, beast and thing

It blasts the trumpet that we heard
As all the world did shake
Moshe Rabbeinu in his hands
Two *luchos* did take

I see the *shofar* in a bush
A ram is snared inside
And Avrohom is thanking God
That worlds did not collide
And though his dear son Yitzchok lived
A ram He did provide

Any sound is acceptable for tekias shofar. Perhaps that it is because to each of us, the shofar may have a different meaning. Perhaps that is why Rav Saadia Gaon's, listing of "Ten Reasons for the Shofar Blowing" is a part of almost every Rosh HaShana Machzor.

And as the *teru'os*
Cry their sounds
Staccato little bursts
My soul it tends to cry with them
As for His love it thirsts

I hear the *Navi* pleading
For his nation to repent
I hear our enemies exult
Triumphantly content

I cry once more while watching
Heart broken like *shevarim*
My eyes I lift, *esah einai*
Esah el heharim

The mighty power of Hashem
I hear it in its blasts
And humbly we fade away
While He forever lasts

I hear the judge, He hearkens me
To stand while He presides
And everything, His eyes do pierce
No matter where man hides

And joyously a blast I hear
Our future has been cast
The sound proclaims that,
"Peace is here"
True *shalom* now shall last

I now hear Eliyahu
The *shofar* in his hand
Proclaiming that *Moshiach*'s here
To bring us to our Land

The blast it sounds,
So loud and clear
As brilliant as the sun
And all the world
Now hears and shouts
"Hashem Echad" as one!

A Mother's Shofar

The days of Sem
Have long since gone
Like the
Yomim Noraim crowd

And what was once
A ritual
By time
Hardly allowed

Indeed I sit
And contemplate
The role
I play today

Torn with great
Uncertainty
No black,
No white
Just gray

Feeling altruistic
Yet
Constraint by
Truth of life
It's hard to be
A sem girl
And
A mother
And a wife

I used to hear
the Shofar's cry
With hundreds of
My friends

And pray so
Very fervently
And swear to
Make amends

The men would sway
And I would pray
In zeal behind the
Curtain

And now alone
I sit at home
A bit confused
Uncertain

He is gone
at 6 AM
A *machzor* drenched
with tears

Of faith and hopes
For family
And all the dreams
He shares

A Yiddishe Momma muses about the days of Seminary that have slipped past her and how, she now plays a different and more important role.

92

With me
The one
Who now stays home
To feed and dress the babies

Filled with questions
Unresolved
The Whats
The Ifs
The Maybes

I'll do my best
And then rush off
With house chores
Some unfinished

And rush to *shul*
With questions
My piety
diminished?

And I'll survive
The dirty looks
As they tug my skirt
And whine

For as I look
Into their eyes
I know
That they're Divine

And as I race
To make it
The shofar blasts
Inside my heart

I hope I hear
The last half
I know
I missed the start

I push upon
The cobblestones
My heart beats like a drummer
My feelings locked
Inside my soul
Confined by *z'man grama*

Indeed the cry of shofar's blast
Replaced by children's cries
I stop and think
And suddenly
I have become the Wise

The future of our destiny
In fact of our nation
Outweighs,
Outshines
The vanity
Of spiritual frustration

I'm not in sem
I'm not alone
I'm here to raise
Tomorrow

To comfort them
To nurture them
Through pain,
Through joy,
Through sorrow

I push my kids
Responsibly
With Dignity
I go

For I have now
A different job
And thus
I need to know

That every blast
That I may miss
Somehow
I'll hear it later

For me
The cries
I hear right now
Are holier
And greater

When I was young
About thirteen
I went somewhere
I'd never been

Cause I grew up
In a small town
Where *bochurim*
Were not around

High Holy Days
Were exactly that
Around the *shul*
The adults sat

A bit of prayer
A bit of chat

They'd talk about
The shofar's sound
We've got the
Loudest blast around

And when I came of age and went
Actually,
I was sent
To a Yeshiva Gedolah
Out of Town
A different level all around

*Bashevkin muses
about his first
Yom Kippur as a
high school boy
in an out of town
Yeshiva Gedolah.It
was very different
than the Young
Israel shul's
davening he was
accustomed to.*

It was Elul
I was scared
Such cries,
Such shouts
I'd never heard

And when I quickly
Finished praying
The other boys
Just stood there swaying

They shrieked and *klopped*
And banged and yelled
I also really
Felt compelled

To follow them
And take their lead
I'd be a *tzaddik*
Yes indeed!

The next *tefilah*
I made sure
I'd be the last one
Out the door

I shook and *shuckled*
Forth and back
Sneaking looks
Keeping track

That I would surely
Finish last
Though I davened
Awfully fast

I'd buy the books
About *Al Chait*
Yom Kippur
I'd anticipate
To *daven* long
And finish late

To *klop* away
And rant and rave
Impressing those
How I'd behave

I'd buy the books
That detail sin
I'll shout and *klop*
Above the din

And then
The next day
In the *shiur*
The *rebbe* spoke
Quite firm
And clear
"Get these
"*Chait* Books"
Out of here

"Stop your looking up
Or at a friend
It's *your* world
You have to mend
Enough *talmidim,*
Of pretend

"There is enough
In each one's heart
To know
Exactly where to start

"If you reflect
On every word
Just you and God
You will be heard

"He is the only One
Whose look
Will care how long
Your *tefilos* took

"He knows just if
The tears you shed
Were meant for Him
Or friends instead"

So as we approach
The *Yom HaDin*
A mind set
You should enter in

The private words
You may confess
Are not for others
To impress

Just from your soul
Just from your heart
It's the only place to start

The Old Jew

*I*n the small *shul* where I daven
Sits an old man in a chair
He's nestled in a corner
His head is bent in prayer

Some say that He is scary
Others say that He is kind
But no matter
What the children say
He never seems to mind

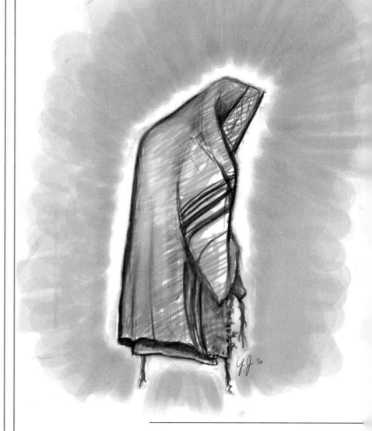

Sometime I see the Ribono Shel Olam treated like an Old Jew nestled in the corner of the Bais Medrash. We all know he's there but somehow we tend to ignore him

They say when He was younger
People flocked to see and pray
And others asked Him questions
And He answered them all day

They stood in awe of
His presence
His advice always sage
But somehow all's forgotten
Swept by time and age

With time
They did forsake Him
As just a memory
And the era of His greatness
Was left to History

Yes, now He is neglected
They all just ignore Him
And when they give him
Some respect
It's only on a whim

Yes, now He sits in solitude
A relic of the past
And the young folk
Oft refer to him
As just "One of the last"

The kids they often mock him
They'll throw a stick or stone
But he just sits
Accepts the shame
Quietly alone

The middle age executives
Have little time to share
The stories of His majesty
They hardly seem to care

They're busy on their cell phones
And some with real estate
But He once owned the property
'Bout which they now debate

They sometimes seem to mock him
As they chat on their cell phone
And they leave him in the corner
Sitting there alone

They say He's not a player
No longer in "the game"
He used to know
But "Hey, things go,"
Cause the "world is not the same"

They're making the decision
When to buy and when to sell
And He sighs there in His corner
Knowing all too well

The old men who once knew him
They still revere His name
They relish in the memories
Of His glory and fame

But even they, too often
Seem not to recall
The days when they revered Him
As He stood so great and tall

Yes, He sits there in the corner
His face it bears a tear
As a few people
Say Hello to Him
Once or twice a year

Yet somehow He remembers th
Though they all forgot
Because He has within Him
What everyone has not

He always will forgive them
Despite what they don't do
He always seems to love them
Yes, each and every Jew

So learn from that old Holy M
What it means to be a Jew
Although that you forgot Him
He does remember you

And as it is within His heart
To forgive what you've forgot
Remember this Yom Kippur

Forget Him Not.

Kol Nidrei Recession Style

*H*eard Beneath the Talis

"Kol Nidrei"
401 (K)

V'esorei
Was Down today

U'Shvuei
My IRA

V'Charomay
My Fannie May

V'Konomai
What can I say?

V'Kinusai, V'Chinuyai
The only way,
I better pray

D'indarnoh
Down by more

U'Dishtabanoh
You just don't wanna

U' d'asarna al nafshasana . . .
I trusted them,
I am a goner

Kool'hone Icharatna B'hon
Regret them all,
I need a loan

Kool'hone y'hon Shoron
Every single stock is gone

... btailin Um'vutalin
Oh! How I've fallen, the margins callin'

Shvikin... Shvisin
I got a fleecin'

B'tailin U'mvutalin
The Ribono Shel Olam's Callin'

Lo Shririn V'Lo kayamin
I got a drummin'...
I had it comin'

Nidrana Lo Nidrei
I know that nothing's here to stay

V'esorona Lo Esorei
And for what we have,
We still must pray

U'shvuasana, Lah Sh'vu'os
What have You done ...
Oy! To us?

I'm praying for yeshuos!

The High Holy Day Season of September 2009 was plagued with scandal after financial scandal and a massive market collapse. With so many people losing their life's savings and investments, Bashevkin thought to imagine what was going on under the individual Talis during the revered Kol Nidrei service.

101

Judgment Day

*T*he *Yom Hadin* is not too far
In fact it's just a week
So I look at the news
To me each day does speak

The world's a mess
I must address
The only thing that's clear
Is that we really have no clue
About the coming year

Like a child's choosing game
Eeny meeny
Miney moe
Who He'll choose
Who'll win or lose
We simply do not know
Eeny meeny miney moe
Where will the stock market go

Fannie Mae
And Freddie Mac
Seems the train
Fell off the track
Will you get
Your money back?

Some were powerful
Some were great
New tycoons of real estate
But they did not anticipate
A market at
The sewer grate

Certain years so many strange events occur. Corruption, scandals and embarrassing events fill the headlines. The lessons of Yom Kippur far transcend the mayhem that was America in the year 2008.

Plunges, rallies
Crashes, peaks
News to us
Forever speaks

Don't ignore!
A lesson learn!
From the Bear
And from the Stearn

Despite our efforts
All our schemin'
AIG
And Shearson Lehman

Poof! Can go
All that you earn
And then to whom
Shall someone turn?

Oil's up
Production's down
What type of storm
Will hit your town?
Giant buildings
Crashing down!

But things that make
The market pale
Troubles on
A greater scale
Do we take
These threats for real?

Kings and despots
Say they'll nuke
Candidates who are
There by fluke
A state led by
A corrupt kook
It's enough
To make you…

…Well
It's enough to
Make you look
Inside that *machzor*
That great book

When you daven
When you say
On that fearful
Judgment Day

The fear-filled
Unesaneh Tokef tale
Tells how fragile
Tells how frail
Rosy faces
All turn pale

Our life
Is in reality
Our wealth
Our health
Mortality

All in our Creator's Hand
Directed by His Master plan
And no one knows
Where he shall land

Where down is up
And up is down
And just His
Holy Sacred Crown
Will forever
Be around

But when we approach
And recognize
That all that's seen
Before our eyes
Is only there
By His great guise
And all one does
And all one tries
Makes him not rich
Nor makes him wise
Therein, my friend,
The secret lies

And thus
I assure you
If that fact is
Plain and true
And if it's clear
Hashem the King
Is in control
Of everything
And only to
His reign
We sing

And if that secret's
Clear to you
In everything
You say and do
This, my friend,
I say to you
Shana tovah
Tikasayvu...

Sukkah Builders

Who will build our *Sukkah*?
I sadly asked my wife
I have not banged a hammer
The last decade of my life

My kids, they used to build it
For them it was a breeze
Chopping wood and banging nails
And sawing down the trees

But now the boys have gone away
Some married, some in Brisk
I'm asked to build the *sukkah* now
But scared to take the risk

And now it's *Erev Yom Tov*
My *aidim*'s very far
And I'm not sure if such a chore
Is in his repertoire

And so I guess I'm here alone
To build it I don't know
Is it crass
To take a class
At the local Home Depot?

I may be good at writing poems
And saying something witty
But put a hammer in my hand
And then you'll start to pity

As my bones get older and my coordination less skilled, the challenge of building the Sukkah mounts, but sometimes it is special new friends that build my Sukkah and teach me how to invite them into the home that they have built for us.

Perhaps I'll get a "Pop-up" one
Which sets up in a snap
Will it fit my family?
A cot to take a nap?

And then I hear a knocking
I see a real gruff kid
A tiny *yarmulke* declared,
"Indeed, I am a *Yid*"

He seemed to look familiar
He lived right down my street
But somehow when I saw him
I kept my thoughts discreet

"Mister, can I help you?
I see you need some aid
I'm quite good at building things
And, please, I won't get paid"

Indeed up went my *sukkah*
In less than half an hour
And suddenly a thought I had
At once began to flower

I said to him, "Please join me
In the *sukkah* you just built"
And suddenly my soul was swept
With many years of guilt

I guess the tale of *Sukkos*
Is bringing *Yidden* close
From the *lulav* and the *esrog*
To the holy words *"ufros"*

For now I have a new guest
My new friend comes each year
He helps us build the *sukkah*
And a *Yom Tov* meal we share

Sometimes to fix a Jewish heart
It takes more than a hammer
To see the beauty of the soul
Without the glitz and glamour

To know a simple wooden hut
Can hold all sorts of Jews
Where they can sit in harmony
And share their lives and *shmooz*

And though I cannot
Saw down wood
Or even bang a nail
I built something
With my new friend
On a much larger scale

For a friendship with
A searching soul
Will warm the freezing cold
And will outlast
The winter winds
For years and years untold

So when you build a *sukkah*
Make sure that there's a space
To find a new *ushpizin*
To occupy a place

For like me you may not know
To drive a nail into wood
But a spark to light the dark
Believe me
      . . . that you could!

107

Still Standing

*T*here's an old *yid* somewhere
in my town
I think he's eighty-three
He's lived not far
From the old *shul*
Since 1923

But no matter how old
That *yid* may be
I know it seems quite strange
The *sukkah* standing
In his yard
Has stood beyond his range

They say it has
Been standing there
Since Wilson did preside
Perhaps it is
The oldest structure
On our town's east side

That *sukkah* stood
Through World War One
Through the Depression, too
And through the years
It stood outside
Inside there sat a Jew

It stood through prohibition
While *Yidden* sneaked *l'chaim*
It stood through
Mockery and doubt
It stood the test of time

Bashevkin enjoys looking at the old Sukkos in the neighborhood that somehow seem to stand all year and never fall despite the rain, wind, snow and storms. They are almost as enduring as the elderly owners who built them years ago.

Though winter's cold
And frigid winds
Rattle its thin sides
The fiercest winds
Could never chill
The shelter it provides

No blinding sun
Of summer fun
Of ancient customs melted
Nor new facades
Of the false gods
Or insults that are pelted

Would break the walls
Of this old hut
And the ancient Jew who's in it
And centuries
Just pass them by
As if they were a minute

Numbers tattooed
On its walls
Its s'*chach* shaken by bombs
The old man returns
And sits each year
Its s'*chach* his fears it calms

And you may laugh
At what I see
"Bashevkin's fascination!"
We do not see
A *sukkah* here
It's your imagination!

There are no *sukkahs* standing there
They're packed in the garage!
A hundred years?
Through dread and tears?
My friend, it's a mirage!

But you may look
In your backyard
And see an empty spot
This *sukkah*, I swear
It still stands there
On *Klal Yisroel*'s lot

And that old man will
Still come back
And take shelter in its walls
He shall return
To wait and yearn
Until *Moshiach* calls

The Toy

*A*nd so the *dreidel*
Spins again
My yarns I spin as well
The *dreidels* of the
Lyrics whirl
A story I shall tell

Of a boy who lived nearby
In a very fancy home
And of the gifts he got this year
Bashevkin writes this poem

Another boy lived next to him
Both parents lost their jobs
And for this very *Chanukah*
No toys, no games, just sobs

The boy who lived
Next door to him
He got this giant toy
A box as big as his garage
I saw him jump for joy!

For in the box, exactly what
That boy cried, he had "needed"
Of everything
He asked his Mom
Nothing went unheeded

Unpacked was a train set
Nintendo, Wii and more
And through the
Window of his house
The boy stared from next door

The custom of Chanukah gelt has morphed into big gifts and presents for some children. Others, seemingly less fortunate can only stare out the window at the neighbor's treasures. But often they find the joy in the simplicity of the spirituality of the Yom Tov and the simplicity of their needs.

He had no Wii, no Gameboy
And would not get a train
But he still had is *lichtilach*
And just would not complain

He knew his parents
Had no work
And not much to be found
But somehow he
Would find the path
For *simcha* to surround

And suddenly his neighbor came
The boy knocked on his door
"Would you like this giant box?
I don't need it anymore."

"Why, thank you," said the little boy
"I'm sure it's lots of fun
I've played with boxes
Times before
But not such a big one!"

Indeed that box
For months was used
A castle… clubhouse… sled…
A clubhouse for the summer days
A tent for his old bed

And well after the fancy toys
Had long gathered their dust
And newer *tchotchkes* had come out
To get them was a must

And batteries
Had long since died
And upgrades
And new versions
And newer models
Did arrive
As nothing but diversions

The little boy with his big box
Had made a lifelong friend
For batteries cannot run out
In the world of let's pretend

And all the neighbors
Play with him
And no one longer mocks
The little boy
Who made his dreams
From a big, old cardboard box

For dreams and aspirations live
Long well beyond a trend
For hope and creativity
Is a boy's most precious friend

For a little light
That's flickering
Lasts way past what it seems
When hope and vision
Transcend toys
And people live with dreams

Miraculous Simplicity

*T*he *Bais Yosef* asked a *kasha*
Tirutzim "*felt nisht ois*"
I know this is a musing
But please just hear my voice
He asked, "If there was oil
To last a single night
Then why eight days of Chanukah
When seven would be right?"

The story of
Chanukah
contains a special
secret that is often
overlooked. It is
the miraculous
simplicity of
nature that we
often take for
granted. That, too,
must be celebrated
on Chanukah.
Here is a new take
on the old question
of the Bais Yosef.

And once I heard an answer
And see it every day
I see it in a family
And kids who sit and play

I see it in the sparkle
Of eyes waiting for *gelt*
I see it in the smiles
Of those who *"gornisht felt"*

I see it in the miracles
Of every single day
Of waking up and washing hands
And then going to pray

I see it in the miracles
Of friends and family
The miracles of luscious smells
And all the world we see

The miracles of livelihood
And all the food we eat
The miracle of having
Enough to make ends meet

The miracle of Earth
And the miracle of Heaven
And now perhaps
We understand
Why add a day to seven

Indeed it was a miracle
The oil lasted eight
But once we thank
Hashem for that
We ought to celebrate

The fact that on day one
A flame indeed did rise
A miracle of burning wicks
Appeared before their eyes

It takes a special wisdom
The *B'nei Binah* did teach
That *Yemai Shemonah* we celebrate
A miracle for each

That even on the first night
Klal Yisroel learns
Indeed it is a *neis* for us
When simple oil burns!

Purim Hopes

Can you imagine
Such a world
Where Purim
Never was

No joy
No hope
No dreams for us
And no euphoric buzz?

Where despair
Would have nowhere
Or hope
To turn around

Where each decree
Would always be
A dire
Judgment found

No Hamans
Would hang
From trees
And good
Would not
Succeed

And never
Would
Great outcomes come
When Mordechai
We'd heed

But my dear friends
Is not the case
As Purim
Was invented

And miracles
They did occur
As we gathered
And repented

And thus
For centuries
We hope
That Purim
Will renew

No matter
What the time
And place
There's hope
For every Jew

That every evil man
There is
And all the evil plots

Can somehow
Turn quite instantly
Like Haman
And his lots

The day of Purim is not 24 hours but 2000 plus years. It represents the dreams and aspirations that every evil decree, vicious enemy, and sordid scheme will dissipate into nothingness. Bashevkin muses about what the Jewish world would be like without a Purim, and blesses the Almighty that it eternally exists.

Yes Purim's
Not a holiday
Where we just
Eat and drink

It's our fate
Eternally
Just take
Some time
To think

It represents
Our every hope
Whenever things
Go sour

That every thing
Can turn around
No matter day or hour

And so we hope
Again this year
A Purim
For us *Yidden*
Where we
Will see
Hung from
A tree
All the Achmajiddin

And all their plans
And all their threats
And every terrorist
Will melt away
On Purim day
And no longer exist

In fact I have a question
Is it silly or profound?
But what did *Yidden*
Do for hope
Before Purim
Came around?

*I*magine that this *Purim*
We have *nahafoch hu*
Where all the world admires
Mordechai the Jew

Imagine that there's no Iran
Who wants to wipe us out
No Hamas and no Fatah
And no UN to spout

Imagine no recession
And stocks are soaring high
Imagine good old Bernie
Was indeed a righteous guy

Imagine all the money lost
Was somehow, someway found
And all the re-found *g'virim*
Would spread their wealth around

Imagine all *rabbeim*
Moros and teachers too
Could teach the children Torah
Without fear of rent due

Imagine that the stimulus
Would bail *yeshivos* too!
And all *meshulachim*
Would not have what to do

Purim is a time of wonder and of miracles. Imagine if the world one day would truly turn around and all things now bitter would turn sweet. A Purim wish from Bashevkin.

116

Imagine there's no hunger
Imagine there's no fear
No need for *Tomchei Shabbos*
No more Kupas Ha'ir

Imagine Haman's grandkids
Learning in Bnei Brak
The *Gemara* said it happened
So this poem is no *hock*

Imagine all the singles
Who write to the *Yated*
Would indeed find their *bashert*
The next one that is *redt*

Imagine Jews in prison
From Yemen to Iran
Would all be freed tomorrow
From Carolina to Japan

Imagine that Obama
Would cut the income tax
Or the judge in Iowa
Would listen to the facts

Imagine that the *Kosel*
Would get the last three walls
Imagine all Jews moving
When that great *shofar* calls

Imagine that Gilad Shalit
Would be sent back to his home
Imagine that this writer
Would end this silly poem

He's really fantasizing
Those dreams are in my head
But perhaps I think
That Purim is
When all dreams can be said

Indeed I hope all wishes
All imagines will come true
And every sad thing
In this world
Will *venahafoch hu*!

When all of *Klal Yisroel* does
What we're supposed to do
We'll laugh at all our *tzaros* past
Venahafoch hu!

And so perhaps this *Purim*
We're *ish lereiyeihu*
And with that sense
Of *achdus* comes
A *Venahafoch hu*

The Boys of Spring

They're coming back
The boys of spring
Each a different tune
He does sing

Some from Brisk
Some from Mir
Some from Toras
Some from Ner

All are special
All are dear
'Specially this time
Of year

Bulging suitcases
Dusty hat
"You can't," yells Mom,
"Go out like that!"

Tons of shopping
Left to do
Clifton,
13th Avenue

After ten
The phone
Does roam
Shmoozing with
The guys
Back home

Sleepy eyes
To shlep
From bed
Negel vasser
Dumped
On head

The "factory"
Is where
They pray
From dawn
To dusk
Goes on all day

In *bais medrash*
Part of day
Then some trip
To get away

But Mom
Needs them
For elbow grease
Shlep the duffel
And valise

Clean the oven
Move the fridge
Sister's is
A *groise nidge*

One of the greatest joys we have as parents is to have the boys come back from Yeshiva before Yom Tov and have them be a part of the frenetic Yom Tov preparations.

Loads of laundry
To be washed
Loads of goodies
To be noshed

But all is worth it
When we see
What *Bnei Torah*
They're to be

Sharing *vertlach*
At the *Seder*
Shir haShirim
Hours later

Chol HaMoed
Breakfast treats
Chapping up
The cakes and sweets

Major breakfasts
Last till noon
And then another
Meal comes soon

But I know
My dearest friends
That even
Bein hazemanim ends

And suitcases
They soon will pack
And wave good-bye
They're heading back

As they wave
They shed a tear
Until they return
Again, next year

*T*he phones were ringing off the hook
In each repairman's store
It was *Nissan*, and once again
They could not ask for more

Indeed they rang with panic
It was that time of year
The servicemen could not be found
No one who would repair

"My oven!" cried Sarah with alarm
It just went on the blink
While Shoshi in St. Louis
Could not drain her kitchen sink

Nechama dumped her broken urn
And bought one that was newer
Ettil was still mopping
The backup from the sewer

And Ruchi down in Boro Park
Said her fridge just won't get cold
How could this happen to me
It's only three weeks old!

Chana's brand new wash machine
Just somehow would not spin
"What should I do with these wet clothes
My cleaning help threw in?"

It seems that every Erev Pesach something always goes wrong. Appliances break or just stop functioning, Washers stop spinning, the sewers back up, and freezers stop freezing. Whatever the disaster, somehow miraculously salvation comes and we all manage a beautiful Seder.

And Bashie in Toronto
Could not bake the cake she made
"Why does potato starch," she cried
Destroy my Kitchen Aid®?"

Food processor will not spin
Please tell me the prognosis
I have so many *seder* guests
I must make more *charoses*!
Oh yes, it's *Erev Pesach*
What worked fine yesterday
Will simply just not turn back on
Or work the proper way!

The *Pesach* ice cream's melting
The freezer does not freeze
The milk is turning sour
And soon it will be cheese!

My washer is not washing
My dryer does not dry
The serviceman he's in no rush
"Next week, I'll come on by"

Itta is in Lakewood
Her voice began to choke
"My table's set for the *seder*
But now a leg just broke"

Hadassah is still crying
From her slight misdemeanor
She plugged it in and it went, Poof!
No more vacuum cleaner!

Said Mimi, "Do not panic
No *Erev Pesach* blues
It's not the vacuum cleaner
I think we blew a fuse!"

The car won't start,
Or worse it crashed
My *bochur*'s still alive
It's just that
He came home last week
And forgot how to drive

But soon the *seder* will begin
And order will soon reign
The fridge will work,
The oven too
And all water will drain

For somehow all the miracles
Arrive for *Pesach* night
And anything
You thought was wrong
Will truly be all right

So, my friends, don't panic
From *Erev Pesach* blues
For soon shall
Come the miracles
Salvation for the Jews

121

A Generation of Frogs

One Morning when
Pharaoh
Woke in his bed
All my kids
That poem have read

And every time
That those frogs jump
In my throat
I get a lump

The joy, the smiles
Sung so bright
Pharoah's pajamas
in the night

Indeed the older
Children moan
When young ones
Sing their silly poem
But it's still with them
As they've grown
And raised
Some children
Of their own

And they forget
Not long ago
Their frogs were jumping
To and fro

From dipping apples
Sweet New Year
Oh M' Darlin'
Do I hear?

And frogs
Were jumping
Everywhere

Yes.
Who knows how
And who knows why
Despite the years
That pass me by

I hear those songs
And start to cry
(A tiny teardrop
In an eye)

Those silly tunes
The little ditty
Sometimes *heartzik*
Sometimes witty

Who knows
The memory it tells
A *Sukkele*
A *Shtetl* Belz

Through
Fire brimstone
Nazi taunts
The melodies
The conscience haunts

We know the ballad
And the tale
The children's cry
Shema Yisrael

That held them close
Despite thick walls
Of monastery's
Austere halls

So
When Pharaoh's frogs
Jump on his nose
Or bite the pimples
On his toes
Or however
That song goes

Don't smirk
Or think that you're
Too smart
Cause all those songs
Became a part
Of memories
That will endure
Like ancient tunes
From days of yore

And when your children
Are all grown
And have some children
Of their own

Once again
From Pharaoh's bed
The frogs will jump
Upon his head

And through the night
With Pharaoh's yell
Your eyes will tear
Your heart will *kvell*

A little child's
Inspiration
Will pass on to . . .

Next generation

I walk the darkened streets
This night
Beneath the moonlight's glow
And in the homes
That I do pass
The children's faces show

To them there is no darkness
To them there's only light
For children of
Our heritage
It is the *seder* night

I walk by homes
Some children sit
And others start to squirm
Despite the winds
That shake the house
The *Yidden* sit there firm

I walk on sandy roads
Of a city once called Goshen
And see the blood
Upon the posts
And unsurpassed
Devotion

"Tonight, my children"
Says the man
"Hashem will set us free
We'll see His word
So often heard
"Pakod pakad'tee"

So many years. So
many sedorim.
So much tragedy.
So much hope.
Imagine how each
seder played out
during its period

I travel in the Holy Land
The *Bais HaMikdash* proud
And thousands
Singing *Hallel*
Their voices sweet and loud

And then comes
Babylonians
And Romans
With their hordes
They try to kill
Our seder night
But all they have are swords

I pass the *Yidden* sent away
On ships now bound for Rome
And hear the fathers
Tell their sons
That one day we'll come home

I pass the caves
This seder night
They sing *Hallel*
As they hide
Eating *Matzah*
Living *Maror*
Children at their side

I walk
The cobblestone-laid streets
An ancient
Persian night
And hear the
Hee sheAmda loud
Despite the dread and fright

No food placed on the dishes
No wine spilled on the table
Just fasting with *emunah*
And thoughts
"Hashem is able"

I pass the cellars
Dimly lit
A secret glow of candles
Outside the home
The rocks are thrown
By hate-filled
Violent vandals

And somehow in Ladino
V'hee sheAmda
A rendition
Forever true
We know the Jew
Outlasts the Inquisition

I walk the paths
In Krakow
In Prague
In Samarkant
And see children
At *Tzafun*
Asking what they want

I walk amongst
The barracks
Of death at Sobibor
And see emaciated
Bodies sit
Huddled on the floor

I know my
Days are numbered
Like digits on my arm
Yet somehow
On this *Pesach* night
I do not fear from harm

And with a certain faith
He sings
Around some
Dried out crumbs
And faintly, I do hear
The hope
As *Dayeinu* he hums

I trudge now toward
Siberia
The path
It still has snow
But warmth
Does calm
The winter chill
When to his son
He'd show

"I know this
Is not *matzah*
But I won't
Eat this bread

For one day
We'll be freed
From here
And eat
Matzah instead"

And as I near my
Humble home
Cars lined up
Round my block

I see inside
Some fancy home
They're looking
At the clock

"Let's move along
And leave Egypt
I'm hungry for the food"
And jokes under
Perched *Yah-mu-kahs*
Display an attitude

And suddenly
My long walk home
4000 years of *Seder*
Makes me wonder
What will be
Just a few more
Decades later

And as I
Open up my door
For Eliyahu *HaNavi*
I know he's seen
All that I saw
Many years before me

He's seen *sedarim*
In the dark
In cells,
Behind barbed wire
To all he comes
And leaves behind
A sense that does inspire

No matter what
The tragedy
Apathy or oppression
We won't forget
The heralded
And beloved expression

That one day all
The tears that flowed
From our tables
To *shamayim*
Will form the path
To lead us back
L'shana haba'ah
B'Yerushalayim

*H*e has the Post-*Pesach*
Matzoh Blues
The one that sat
They did not use

He sits so sad inside the box
A few friends and some crumbs
He mourns his fate and wonders why
With questions and "How comes?"

How come I was not chosen?
Why was I left for later?
I was so crisp and crunchy
Yet not used for the *seder*!

I'm not the extra pound they bought
I was from the *chaburah*
Carefully they baked me
From flour that was *shmurah*
But I fared better than my friend
Did you hear the sad *besurah*?

They took him on the last day
So pure and sweet and *aidel*
And ground him up and added eggs
And he became a *kneidel*

I sit now after *Pesach*
As I ponder my mixed luck
I was not used on Pesach
Yet me they did not *bruck*

Do you ever wonder what the leftover matzah feels like. sitting alone in the box? What about every unused mitzvah item. Bashevkin muses as to what is going on inside that matzah's head.

128

The box is dark and lonely
A tear forms in my eye
I was not used on *Yom Tov*
I slowly start to cry

My tears may wet the *matzah*
I begin to fear
But now it's after *Yom Tov*
No one will even care

And then a smile starts to form
Although it is quite feeble
Perhaps this *Shabbos* I'll be used
For liver, *ayr mit tzveeble*

Maybe *seudah shlishis*
When they've run out of *challah*
"Use me!" I'll shout,
"For your *seudah*"
They'll hear me as I holler

Or maybe shmeared
With cream cheese
In Chaiml's knapsack
Or in Eli's lunch bag
I know they will
Come back

And open up my box
And find some use for me
A snack, a lunch, or I'll just wait
Perhaps *Pesach Sheini*!

Sometimes we're not chosen
We sit inside and mope
We want to be a part of it
And all we do is hope

But each one has a *tachlis*
It's his turn for a bite
And when you're chosen
For your job
I guess that time's just right…

129

The Terminal

*T*he terminal
Is hardly still
In fact,
The place is teeming
Some sad good-byes
Some mixed with cries
Strollers,
Babies screaming

They're going back
They're going home
Depends on your perspective
Nary an eye
Is to be dry
Yet all of them reflective

Suitcases
Some held with glue
some taped with cellophane
Some overweight
And "Oy! I'm late!"
"How will I make the plane?"

People getting nervous
Some try to sneak in front
"You know, I have a plane to make,"
They shriek when I confront

Security checks
As he inspects
"Did you pack this alone?"

Watching the scenario at the El Al terminal after Yom Tov evokes tears and smiles. Join Bashevkin as he quietly watches and muses in the background.

"Of course we did!
It's for our kid!
It's not the first he's flown!"

Suitcases both large and small
Stickers, labels, tags
Corrugated boxes packed
And large green duffel bags

"Excuse me, sir
This one's too large
And this one it's too heavy

"You know the rule
The cost of fuel!
We must issue a levy!"

"Can you take this package?
My son it's his great wish
Don't tell a soul
It's just a roll
My wife's gefilte fish!"

"My *shaifeleh*
She's leaving
My *einiklach* in tow
I really can't imagine why
I ever let her go"

Indeed the sights
And sounds of it
Can make a grown man cry
Especially if it's his kid
Who's now waving goodbye

I know it's hard
To board that plane
We'd really love to stay
But wait!
We still are smiling
There's a six hour delay!

Eternal Avos

Come join me for a journey
For six weeks, if not more
A journey that begins back when
Back in days of yore

It started back at Sinai
From Hashem to Moshe's ears
Those very words
Remain with us
Passed down through the years

Passed to Yehoshua
The *Z'kainim* and *Nevi'im*
Anshei K'nesses Hagedolah
Roshei Sanhedrin and *N'ssim*

It's been our compass
Through dark roads
It's been our ray of hope
The beacon that does guide us when
Through golus paths we grope

Of how to judge a fellow Jew
Or how to serve our master
Or when friendships that are so untrue
Can lead to a disaster

About an attitude toward work
And to all of those who love us
And how to always remember
That there is
One above us

And *derech eretz* has its place
Respective to the Torah
And how we'd live in anarchy
(of course *ilmalei mora'ah*)

And when to speak
And when to *shveig*
And when one is *goilem*
Torah, Avodah, Gemilas Chasadim
The pillars of the *Oilam*

48 Ways to Torah
How to make wisdom last
Lessons from a floating skull
And how the tongs were cast

They teach us how to daven
How to eat and drink
About nature and the government
And how we are a link

They join us in our living room
Or at a shiur in *shul*
They are with us no matter what
Grade we are in school

They teach us that this lavish world
Is just a corridor
And not to dismiss or be remiss
To someone meek and poor

What is Torah etiquette
How not to interrupt
And not to try to befriend those
Who we know are corrupt

Who is a student of Avrohom
And who soars like an eagle
Who wears a crown
Of a good name
From all that is most regal

In triumph over enemies
They taught us not to gloat
And each one has a unique thought
A teaching he would quote

To not judge if you're alone
And who is really rich
And he who lives near *chachomim*
Should not be paid to switch!

Do not waste your precious time
Don't sleep away your days
About the *kinyan* Torah
And its forty-eight ways

These words they are not history
Or tales from yesteryear
They are alive and relevant
Each and every year

Make sure that you invite them
Each *Shabbos* in your home
The power of their messages
Transcends this simple poem

For those who talk to us each week
Are Fathers who did love us
They handed down a holy crown
We know as *Pirkei Avos*

133

*H*e walked into the *seforim* store
A place all filled with books
He could not find what he looked for
So he still looks and looks

The days of *Sefirah* have arrived
A time to lift the soul
And so the *mocher seforim* tries
To justify his role

"Perhaps you want *sifrei mussar*
Or *shmiras halashon*
A *sefer* from a *mashgiach*
A tape from Paysach Krohn?"

The young man blushes just a bit
He tells the *seforim* seller
"That truth be told
I wish you sold
A CD
A cappella

"This way I'll listen in my car
'Cause that is where I'll play 'em
I know that it is *Sefirah* now
And so, no FM, AM!"

And then he saw the new CD
No music, just a drum
With doo-wop sound
And *klops* abound
A bunch of guys who hum

During the mourning period of sefirah, Many try to entertain themselves while attempting to abide by the spirit of sefirah, Indeed they opt to abstain from listening to live music, opting instead for a capella CDs. But do we sometimes forget the reason for the mourning period and neglect to address that most important theme?

He picked it up and smiled
He saw it had his song
To his dismay
He could not pay
The line was just too long

And so he pushed his way ahead
And tried to cut the line
When someone looked at his CD
He yelled, "Excuse me! That is mine!"

The fellow who just got pushed
Did not become perturbed
He said, "My friend
Can you defend
Why you are so disturbed?"

"Oh! I must to get back to my car
The meter's running out
I only have one thing to buy!"
He began to shout

"All these people
Here in line
They seem to have all day
So let me through
And I mean you
Because I want to pay!"

The old man stared pathetically
And stroked his graying beard
He tried to calm the young man's nerves
(I really think he cared)

"Is it not the time of *Sefirah*
Your music, can't it wait?"
The young man shouted back at him
And then became irate

"This tape it has no music!
It's all within the law!
And so your little 'comment'
Perhaps you should withdraw!"

The old man asked so softly
A voice quite hard to hear
His tone was soft and pleasant
His heart seemed so sincere

"Why do we not hear music?
Why don't we sing or dance?
Can you please explain it
Can you give me a chance?"

The young man laughed quite heartily
"Some students they all died!
Just what are you driving at"
His tone was awfully snide

The older man said softly
"Why did they pass away?
Do you know the reason
That music we don't play?"

With CD in his hand to buy
The young man said, "I do
The *talmidim* were punished
Kavod lo nahagu"

"I see," replied the graying m
"Somehow they lacked respec
Perhaps it is a time to think
And act in circumspect

"For if we push in line or shou
Or *shtuch* another fella
Do you think that all is cured
With a dose of a cappela?

"It's not just about the music
Or the songs that we don't sin
It's counting toward *Har Sinai*
And how to meet the King

"It's about Rabbi Akiva
BaTorah, klal gadol
It's about the virtues of our pe
We all look to extol

"And so I do apologize
If I irked you in some way
About the CD that you were
Just about to play"

The young man turned and
Slowly walked
He really took his time
And he came back with no CL
But *Kisvei Chofetz Chaim*

Rahbee Shimon bar Yochai

*T*he supreme of *Tanaim*
Greatest in the mind's eye
The talmid of Rav Akiva
Rahbee Shimon bar Yochai

The depth of his great learning
Where secrets therein lie
Toras niglah venistar
Rahbee Shimon bar Yochai

To speak the truth of Roman deeds
Somewhere there was a spy
And so he had to flee and hide
Rahbee Shimon bar Yochai

In a cave they sat and hid
As twelve years passed them by
Rav Elazar and the great
Rahbee Shimon bar Yochai

In sand they buried their bodies
From foot 'till near the eye
Immersed in Torah totally
Rahbee Shimon bar Yochai

A stream appeared to give them drink
A carob food supply
To nurture the existence of
Rahbee Shimon bar Yochai

The world celebrates the Yahrzeit of Rabbi Shimon Bar Yochai on Lag BaOmer. Many ballads and joyous memorial songs were written in honor of this great sage. For the English speaking public, Bashevkin tries one of his own, containing allusions to the Talmud in Shabbos 33b, K'subos 77 and Yerushlami Sanhedrin 1:3.

And when they left their holy cave
They could not just comply
With a mundane world of work
Rahbee Shimon bar Yochai

For all frivolities of life they burned
A look from a holy eye
Until Heaven called out to them
Rahbee Shimon bar Yochai!

"To destroy the world I made
Your actions do imply
Return back to your holy cave!
Rahbee Shimon bar Yochai"

And then they saw a simple Jew
Hadasim held so high
Symbolize *Zachor V'Shamor*!
Rahbee Shimon bar Yochai

"How precious are Your children!"
He looked up toward the sky
And so he came back to this world
Rahbee Shimon bar Yochai

And with him came the Zohar
The secrets from on high
That we share with utmost fear
Rahbee Shimon bar Yochai

And all the while with us
No rainbow in the sky
For his merit would protect
Rahbee Shimon bar Yochai

To release the world
From judgment
He could do with one cry
He and Elazar his son
Rahbee Shimon bar Yochai

"Your greatness," said Rav Ak
"Know just Hashem and I
For you transcend
The greatest men,
Rahbee Shimon bar Yochai"

And every year they travel
To Har Meron on high
They sing and sway
All night they pray
Rahbee Shimon bar Yochai

And the sun shines inspired
As thousands say goodbye
Yoet their souls are duly fired
By *Rahbee* Shimon bar Yochai

A Battle For The Ages

$\mathcal{A}$ battle for the ages
That thundered way on high
With angels and seraphim
Who asked Almighty, "Why?

"Is there a man amongst us
What is his business here?
Let him stay back down on earth
And do his dealings there."

Hashem said "for my Torah!
He's come to bring it down
'Naaseh V'Nishmah' his people cried
With each word worth a crown!"

"Why give your precious Torah
To man who's born of Eve?
With foibles and all sorts of flaws
Who'll lie, cheat and deceive

"Generations before humans
Nine hundred seven four!
Why send it down to mortal man
Please leave it! We implore!"

And so the humble messenger
The shaliach from Hashem
Was told by the Creator
"Why don't you answer them?"

The epic battle between Moshe and the angels for the right to receive the Torah is documented in Shabbos Perek Rabbi Akiva. Bashevkin takes snippets of that Gemara and portrays it in poetry.

"Almighty, *Aibishter*!" he cried
To answer I aspire
But they shall open up
Their mouths
And burn me with their fire!"

Replied Hashem,
"Do not fear them!
I'll shield my servant, loyal
Just hold the *Kisai HaKovod*
So holy and so royal"

It has the face of your forebear
Yes, Yaakov's face etched in
Who battled with a *Malach*, too
And he, indeed did win

And so the humble of all men
Told the Angelic crew
"Please let me ask some questions
They'll only be a few…"

"This Torah that you'd like to keep
Its holiness you crave
Does it say somewhere in Shmos
That you were once a slave?"

"The fellow who I battled with
His name, you may not know
For none of you encountered
The vicious King Pharoh

"And what else does
The Torah write
Don't kill, don't steal, don't lie
Have you ever had a *din Torah*
Way up here, up on high?

"Mothers must you honor?
Or fathers to respect?
Or flaws in character have you?
That *mussar* shall perfect?

"Do you need a *Shabbos* rest?
Are angels sometimes jealous?
Is Torah law addressed to you?
For if it is, please tell us

And so *Malachim* said,
"You're right!
Please take this holy gift"
And each one gave a *matana*
To show there was no rift

Indeed they all presented
Malach Hamaves too
The secret of *k'tores*
To save a dying Jew

"Indeed my job in Heaven
Is to bring the souls back home
To learn the Torah way up high
Beneath the Heaven's dome"

But this gift that I give you
Extends the life below
For that is where the Torah lives
Your lesson, I now know

And so our Master Moshe
Brought Hashem's word
Down to earth
For all *Yidden*
To revel in
Its immeasurable worth

More than we can imagine
A gift from High Above!
Appreciate, this *Chamudah*
Given with His love

Chaim'l on Shevuos

I look around the *bais medrash*
It's a little bit past one
He brought along young Chaim'l
Who thought "this will be fun!"

And Chaim opens his *Chumash*
And points to *Alef Bais*
Reading each line carefully
For this he waited days

*Sometimes it is the
youngest children
on Shavuos night
who outdo, and
thus inspire us
older folk to
continue learning*

His father cracks a smile
"When will he close his eyes?"
But Chaim says "I'll learn all night
Until the sun will rise"

And not too far from his wide eyes
Sway seventeen-year-olds
Who *shukel* with their giant tomes
As *Rashi's p'shat* unfolds

And *bochurim* with coffee cups
They argue with their thumbs
An old man sitting 'cross the way
Smiles as he hums

And then they see the little boy
Who reads "what *rebbi* said"
And wonder, "What's he
   doing here?
Should he not be in bed?"

An hour's worth of *Alef Bais*
The clock approaches two
And Chaim and the *bochurim*
Their missions they pursue

And as the clock approaches three
An old man checks for dawn
The boys are speaking softly now
As each one gives a yawn

And as the darkness dissipates
And the morning star does rise
The shouts in learning falter as
The boys all rub their eyes

They look upon the large wall clock
Each looks back at his wrist
They struggle to think clearly now
As slumber they resist

Yet nuzzled in a corner sways
Chaim with his *siddur*
Holding it as if he were
The last Torah transmitter

The boys are getting tired now
The old man starts to *shmooz*
Two tired fellows sneak in back
And take a little snooze

And Chaim'l keeps trudging on
For he's not had enough
And as the dawn begins to rise
He shouts the letter *tof!*

But no one seems to hear him
Their minds are all asleep
It's Chaim'l, his *Alef Bais*
Our *mesorah* to keep

For when the big boys
Tire out
And old men seem quite worn
The Chaimls will bear the torch
To our next *Shavuos* morn

A Long Three Weeks

*A*nd at the start of
Summer fun
Comes three weeks of
The laughs undone

As walls are breached
And Temples burned
And lessons preached
But hardly learned

Perhaps in joy
It sets a tone
That there is no
Tragedy unknown

For plans of fun
That's filled
With pleasure
Clearly one
Must stop and measure

And as the summer
Begins this year
It starts with a
Collective tear

Slid down the face
Community
Down the cheek
Calamity

And though each one
Will go his way
Some to swim
And some to play

The start that tells
Of siege and breach
The 17th begins
To teach

That three weeks are
A part of life
And until they're gone
We live with strife

Of course,
Three weeks
Will pass once more
And summer's fun
Like times before

Will fade the memories
Of fasting
With songs and cheers
That seem long-lasting

But forget thee not
That these three weeks
Each day to us
So softly speaks

The three weeks of Summer 2008 began with many tragedies, just a reminder that this period of time even nestled in a summer setting cannot escape its tragic destiny.

144

And glasses cracked
At joyous times
The memories
Of *churban* chimes

Forget it not
In color war
That we always wish
For something more

And when we swim
And when we boat
In our minds
Serenely note

Our mouths can't fill
With summer fun
Until the winter
Will be done

And sun that shines
Will clearly say
"Schok Pinu,
       ... *Ahz yimalei"*

Birah Tochiach

Week number two
What can you do?
Moshiach's still not here
We ask for him
So many times
But do we really care?

Try to think hard
What is the card?
That indeed will bring *Moshiach*
Don't use *sevara*
Open a *Gemara*
And read *"Birah Tochiach!"*

For *aveiros*
The "Big Three"
Years of *galus*
Seventy
But what's with the
Bayis Sheini?
That burned from hate
And we still wait
Don't need to get too brainy

We all try *segulos*
To bring *yeshuos*
But the *Gemara* says just why
It's been a while
We're in denial
So the next weeks I will try

Every year before Tisha B'Av, we have to reflect on ways to fight the Sinas Chinam that destroyed our Bais HaMikdash. Bashevkin offers some ideas for Ahavas Chinam.

To look Above
And find some love
For every single *yid*
It's not easy
I can feel queasy
Myself, I do not kid

Maybe make
A giant sign
A massive *kol korei:*
"Don't push in line!"

"Don't double park
Your car today"
"Give someone
The right of way"

To the space
You will not beat her
And put a quarter
In her meter

Yes, fortitude
Is very tough
Who said that this
Is simple stuff?

Matzav, Yated
Yeshiva News
For *chessed*
It surely can be used

Give a ride
A simple deed
Help a Jew
Who is in need

147

(Don't charge the man
If you can pay
Or if you're going
Anyway)

Pass a hospital
Stop on in
Try and make
A *choleh* grin

I know you do not
Know the guy
Ahavas chinam
That is why!

Did you ever
Make a *minyan*
For someone with no friends?
I don't mean for a *siyum*
I mean for
When life ends

When no one knows
Who you may be
You're masked
With anonymity

Be *menachem avel*
Someone you don't know
Take the time
To share their pain
Nechama to bestow

It will show we really care
And not just for our friends
Visit in a nursing home
A place where life descends
Sit and let them tell their tales
Before their soul ascends

Tzipisah liyeshuah
The question they will ask
Perhaps it's more than waiting
To satisfy this task

It may be *ahavas chinam*
For hatred's great amends
Unadulterated love ensures
That this long *golus* end

Heed The Call

*H*e stood there almost all alone
And tried to warn the folk
But no one turned his ear or heart
To all the words he spoke

He spoke about their actions
About impending doom
But they were split in factions
And in their hearts no room

For all the *mussar shmuessen*
That Yirmiyahu railed
And all his strong *tochacha*
Sadly it had failed

They saw not signs he showed them
The breach in that great wall
They never thought they'd see the day
The *Bais Mikdosh* would fall

And then they went to exile
And sent across the seas
And soon they got used to it
And did not hear the pleas

When he cried to them as Spaniards
"Your life here is too rich"
And lo their lives
Were comfortable
Their ways
They would not switch

The Navi Yirmiyahu warned and warned and yet the Jews turned a deaf ear. The Bais HaMikdash was destroyed and we were sent into exile. How often does the call go out for teshuva in our day? Do we heed the call?

149

They saw not signs
He showed them
The Church would have its way
They thought not Inquisition
Torquemada, auto-de-fe

And then he cried in Poland
Is there respect for *shul*?
And lo their ways
Were comfortable
They took him for a fool

They did not hear the hoof beats
Of Cossacks on the loose
And all the *divrei mussar*
They seemed of no good use

And then he cried in Germany
"Of Berlin what's become"
But they all felt enlightened
"The redemption has begun!"

They did not hear the broken glass
Or see the brown shirts *"Heil"*
It was again for us to drink
The *navi*'s cup of bile

And as we sit again quite smug
Do we not hear his voice
When we have opportunities
Do we make the right choice?

Do we see the missiles
Of a madman in Iran

Or friends who may soon turn
To justify their plan?

As this year's *Tisha B'Av* arriv
Are we listening to shouts?
A *novi* cries through the even
Yet we still have our doubts

Are these signs for *teshuvah*?
Are these calls to heed?
Are we listening to all the sig
That seem to shout and plead

Your nation is in danger
It's time to heed the call
So that again the holy walls
Never shall they fall

So listen to the world around
Ignore the silly news
And heed the call specifically
The things that talk to Jews

And if we listen carefully
And rip our hearts in pain
Not ever shall a *Tisha B'Av*
Bring sadness once again

For it will transform
A source of joy
With *teshuvah* our preemptior
For *Tisha B'Av* we'll all rejoice
With imminent redemption!

150

"How Much More?"

*T*his week I asked
My little boy to write
He jotted this
Without a fight

"On *Tisha B'av*
We sit on the floor
We stare at the *kinnos*
And ask,
'How much more?'"

What he meant
I am not sure
"But, *Ribbono Shel Olam*
How much more?"

Nero, Vespasian
And Titus
That was just
The start for us

The false *Moshiach*
On the cross
No one thought much
About his loss

But no peace came
From "talk of love"
Hate is what
His world's made of

From Hadrian (76-138)
To Constantine (337)
Decrees and acts
So cruel and mean

Islam's founder (571)
From desert sands
Agonized with
His demands

His followers, now
Are all the same
The infidels
Shall take the blame

Pope Gregory (540)
And Charlemagne (742)
Were vehicles
Of tortured pain

Paris in 1242
Louis thought he
Surely knew
How to destroy
The eternal Jew

Every *Shas*
He'd get and burn
Tried to destroy
All that we learn

No peace from
England's Edward One (1290)
He made sure
The Jews were gone

Each one he surely
Would expel
350 years
Until Cromwell

Martin Luther (Germany 1483)
Faked being nice
His vitriol
Soon turned to ice

And so his hatred
He would rant
No difference
Catholic, Protestant

No peace
For Jews in Spain (1450-1500s)
From Isabella's
Wretched reign

Torquemada's
Auto-de-fe
How many Jews
Did they burn each day?

Indeed the list
Goes on and on
From Czars to kings
To popes named John

With names that you
And I don't know
Except the end
"Yemach shemo!"

Commies, Nazis
Jihadists
We can compile
Lists and lists

Crusades
Pogroms
And Blood libels
Forgeries
And made-up Bibles

Protocols
Of so-called "Zion"
Tomes of hatred
Filled with lyin'

Iraqi *Yidden*
Hung for spying
Tortured just
For not complying

Stalin's Gulag
Herman Goering
Hundreds of millions
Upon us warring

Numbers tattooed
With the Lie
That the *"Arbeit*
Macht unz frei"

What did we get
To set us free
Barbed wire
And Zyklon B

Gas Chambers
And vicious dogs
Human flesh
As soap and logs

The world forgets
Does not ask "why?"
Then they all
Start to deny

Trampling on
The poor and downtrodden
The boots of
Jihad's Bin-Laden

And don't forget
More decimation
The golus of
Assimilation

All of them
They wish us gone
But You insist
We carry on ...

Miraculously
We persevere
For Rome is gone
BUT WE ARE HERE!

So look at the *kinnos*
As you sit on the floor
But look up to Heaven and ask
"How much more?"

Two thousand years
Yisrael's pain
Fettered by that
Golus chain

Break the bonds
And show Your reign
With Moshiach and *geulah*
Venomar 'Amein!'

Nachamu, Nachamu

*A*s ancient tears
Begin to dry
And others start anew
I hear a voice
A'calling
With not one word but two

A voice that travels
With us
Consoling us times two
A voice that says
"Nachamu, ami
Dear children, *nachamu"*

From the 9 *Av*
Of *meraglim*
And they saw not the next day
And all the ones
Who cried out
Would slowly pass away

With His mercy
On the fifteenth
The Jews arose anew
And heard the
Consolation
Nachamu, nachamu

Alas, we entered
Yisroel
But *tzaros* found there, too
Nevuchadnetzar
Hadrian
And Titus and his crew

The double expression Nachamu, Nachamu represents to me the constant, ongoing consolation that Jews need to survive the endless onslaught of the misery called galus. Only a double dose of Divine consolation can help us endure until the final nechama.

They pillaged us
And ransacked
And burned down the *Heichal*
Yet Rabi Akiva
Saw the fox
On his face a *shmeichel*

"*Rebbe*," asked his students,
"Why have
A smile on your face
When you see desolation
In this great and holy place?"

"Don't worry, my *talmidim*,
This fox it speaks to you
Those words fulfilled
Means He will build
My children, nachamu"

And when they put us
All in chains
And carried us in boats
Imprisoned us
In fortresses
Guarded by deep moats

Yet some indeed
Escaped, survived!
Perhaps forebears of you
And as they ran
They heard the voice
Nachamu, nachamu

And they tied us
To the rack
And torched auto-de-fe
And then with
Our families
The monsters had their way

But here we are as remnants
Whom they failed to subdue
Whose parents
Heard a calling
My children, nachamu

When hordes of Cossacks
They did roam
With pogroms, hate and libels
And bore the cross
Of perfidies
While raising "Holy Bibles"

And through it all
We persevered
When they yelled, "Kill the Jew"
For in our hearts
We heard the voice
That whispered "*Nachamu*"
They tattooed
On the shriveled arms
That bore our sacred *tefillin*
No sound was heard
The world, no word
While those ghastly beasts
Were killin'

And no one, sure
Would ever think
That once more we'd renew
Except the ones
Who heard Him call
My children, nachamu

And somewhere in
A prison cell
There sits a lonely Jew
Who knows not why
They took him there
Or what they plan to do

And as he sits
Confined alone
In a room without a view
The words he knows
Will free his soul
My children, nachamu

As each one has their *tzara*
For *golus* has no friends
And as we wait so tearfully
until this golus ends

Don't despair my brothers
There's hope for me and you
When sons and fathers
Sing and dance

. . . "Father, Nachamu"

"*C*haim Yankel!"
She shouted
"WHAT ARE WE GONNA DO?"
"*Vos eppes?*"

"*VOS EPPES?*
IT'S SOON *NACHAMU!*

"We can't stay in the city
In the sweltering heat
Someone may see us!
Who will we meet?

"What kind of picture?
What kind of *ponim?*
Imagine it leaks
To all the *shadchanim!*

"We'll *shlep* to the country
With our *maidels* and *yingels*
We'll find a hotel
That doesn't have singles!"

"But my car
It's *tzubrochen!*
It has a flat tire"
"I don't care
We are going
You think I'm a *freier?*"

Shabbos Nachamu is the highlight of the summer season. Everyone and their brother-in-law seems to be running to the country to celebrate the end of the three weeks. Bashevkin peeks in on one Brooklyn couple's attempt to make it up to the Mountains.

"We'll hitch us a ride
With some other fellow
Who's going to Woodridge
Perhaps Monticello!

"I think there's a concert
Instead of a race
Whatever it is
I'm out of this place!

"Imagine they hear
We stayed in the city
A *groise rachmanus*
What a *shandeh*! A pity!

"We'll rent a big van
And then stay 'till Monday
If we're not there for *Shabbos*
at least go on Sunday!"

Chaim Yankel kept quiet
he put up his hand
"One minute, my dear
I don't understand!"

"Last Sunday,
I think
The *Bais Hamikdosh*
Burned down
So why the big rush
To get out of town?

"At last recollection
We're still stuck
In *golus*
And *Yidden* are mired
In all sorts of *tzorus*

"Of course a small break
Is our objective
But let's give this *Nachamu*
The right perspective

"We need a *nechama*
For the *churban* today
But who says we'll get it
By running away?

"And spending a fortune
Shmoozing with friends
And catching the drift
On all the new trends
While looking to see
What everyone spends?

"So let's just stay home
And shut off the phone
We'll have the whole city
All for our own!"

Here Comes The Sun

I remember it like yesterday
Oh! How the world has changed
What is considered normal now
Back then was called deranged

Yet through it all, decades gone by
Something's remained as one
So let's all say, two weeks away
Boruch… Here comes the sun

It cycled round the Heavens
Five – Six – Seven – Years
Each night it slips
Under the earth
And then it reappears!

And once again, its path renews
No matter what we've done
Indeed my friend, we don't know much
Except… here comes the sun

And in those years
That have gone by
Since last it passed this way
The world's become
A sadder place
Despite your shining ray

So many left who led us
Gedolei Yisroel
For last time's prayer we had them here
And in our presence dwell

Every twenty eight years, a special blessing is made when the sun is at its peak in the cycle of creation. Bashevkin wrote this in late March of 2009 in anticipation of his second Birchas haChamah. And he reflected that perhaps as much as the sun has stayed the same, so many aspects of the world have changed. But, no matter what happens in the world, we are still around ready to bless the Almighty as …

159

Rav Shach, Rav Shlomo Zalman
Rebbes, Bobov and Ger
Rav Moshe and Rav Yaakov
Rav Pam, Rav Schwab, Rav Shneur

The Steipler and Rav Hutner
And dozens, dozens more
Rav Gifter and Rav Boruch
And Rav Gedaliah Schorr

They left us their *talmidim*
And rays from their own sun
And you, the *Shemesh* in the sky
Saw every single one

And they all stood across
The world
So different, yet as one
They looked on high and
Thanked Hashem
With the blessing of the sun

Yes, things have changed,
And not for good
Since back in '81
And we're to blame,
Yet you're the same
Boruch… Here comes the sun

You saw newfangled toys arrive
The stuff we did not need
Your miracles outshone them all
In growing food from seed

The last time that
We blessed the sun
We played records, cassettes
No MP3 and no CD
How quickly one forgets

Cell phones were for the elite
Officials or those "better"
The last time that
We blessed the sun
We still could write a letter

Plastic cards to get you cash?
And some to create debt?
Mice would scare us all back th
What was the internet?

And yet somehow we manage
To get what we got done
But you stood there
And thought "Beware!"
Boruch… Here comes the sun

Tylenol was never thought
To perhaps be cyanide
A terrorist would indeed kill
But without the suicide

There was a method to the madr
Diane and Charles still smiled
There was no label,
"Kids-at-risk"
Those days they called 'em, wi

160

Airplanes watched
You as they flew
But many are since gone
Pan Am is bust, Eastern is dust
But you keep shining on

When we last said "hello" to you
And thanked the great Creator
Ma Bell owned every phone
With a real live operator!

Russia's grip was still real strong
Iran warred with Iraq
We'd said "forever Gush Katif
We'll never give it back!"

Cars were big, and gas had lead
No shuttles flew to space
No one heard of Lockerbie
While you still stood in place

For you were here and glowing
No matter who was on the run
A *bracha* we are owing…
Boruch Hashem
    … Here Comes the Sun

I remember it as bright as you
I stood right by Rav Shneur
I heard the *bracha* of hundreds
With voices loud and clear

There were so many of us
And yet we stood as one
"Osei maaseh bereishis"
Oh yes… Here Comes the Sun

Almost three decades later
We're less, in some ways, more
As we gather once again to pray
And ask, perhaps implore

That as we look
Toward Heaven
Where our eyes and prayers
Do soar
And reaffirm Creation
That we often ignore

I hope that I will make it
The next time it shines here
I hope my children take me then
As I took them this year!

Let's all add one *tefillah*
Next time this *bracha's* said
The world will be a better place
With *Moshiach* at its head

And all the world will recognize
The sun which stands on high
Is just a pawn devised by He
The One Who rules the sky

The sun looks down
Upon the earth
And lets out a great sigh
To reminisce at sin and bliss
The years that passed it by

"I saw the man's creation
I saw the *Yidden's* rise
And then I saw destruction
The tears and endless cries

"I saw the Romans
Breach the walls
And Spain's auto de fé
And somehow
I still had the strength
To shine another day

I saw the flames of Auschwitz
And *Yidden* burned alive
Survivors saw
That I still shone
They knew that they'd survive

They thought I'd never rise aga
After 1945
Despite the darkness of that nig
We both somehow survive

And now I see *geulah*
As I perform what He has wille
And let new light
Now shine for them
With *ohr haganuz* filled …

Summer's Breeze

Camp Confusion

I'd like to make
A camp this year
It'll be my claim to fame
They say the main thing
You must do
Is find a proper name

I need a name
To give it
A name that is unique
A name that
Lends excitement
And all the people speak

"Did you hear
About the camp
That's truly number one?
The name they say
Is special
The name it is
Camp Fun!"

But no! I cannot
Give that name
I think I am mistaken
That name, my friends
Is not unique
It is already taken

And so with friends
I gather
Together we would *hock*
To find something original
We'll call it
Camp Geshmak

Perhaps that's
Not original
I need a special brand
Perhaps I'll name it
Camp-So-Sweet
Or maybe "Candyland"

Again, they say
It's taken
Hasogas g'vul's the *p'sak*
And so I'll choose
Another name
Perhaps we'll say
Camp K'nock

That may be
All too powerful
For kids dandy and fine
Maybe I should
Try a name
And call it Camp Sunshine?

*Bli Ayin Horah,
there are so many
wonderful camps.
Obviously, each
one needs
a unique name.
Bashevkin muses
about all sorts of
names… and the
possibilities are
endless.*

Or something dainty
For the tots
I'll name it something grand
Like Rainbow
Princess, Rakeves
Or maybe Kinderland

Those names, you say
Are taken too?
Oh please don't make a fuss
If I just start
Another camp
And name it Kids R' Us

You mean to say
That's taken?
I really did not know
Perhaps I'll make
A travel camp
Perhaps "Boys On The Go"

And for the girls
Chaveiros
Or maybe Raninu
Do you like
Sameiach
Perhaps Yedidos too?

And for all the big
"*Machers*"
I'll make a camp the best!
And name it for
Its excellence
I will call it Camp Fest!

Well, that surely
Did not sit well
I just heard from the owner
I'm sorry that
Is taken
And so is Kanfei Yonah!

So I ponder
My camp's name
Seems every name's in use
And I cannot
Just borrow one
And new I can't produce!

Oh! What a problem
We should have
An Americana *tzarah*
But seeing all the
Camps out there
I'll call mine...
Kain Ayin Hara!

My Country

My Country Tis Of Thee, Sweet Land of Liberty ... and Monticello and Woodbourne and Loch Sheldrake and South Fallsburg and Ellenville, too!

I'll share with you a story
My neighbor swore it's true
It did not happen yet with me
Perhaps it did with you

My friend, he went last summer
To New York's DMV
And stood in line behind a man
Who came from Willy B.

The man, he sure stood out in there
You sure would not have missed him
The first time at the DMV
He did not know the system

He had to deal with a new clerk
He said her name was Shawna
She clearly, also, never met
A *Chasid* in her corner

The man who came from Williamsburg
His license was a mess
The problem really came to light
When she asked him his address

Bashevkin always gets a kick of the fact that the Catskill Mountains was called "The Country. It really hit home after reading in a prominent Jewish periodical how a parent lamented that the first telltale signs that her child was going off the straight and narrow path was when he referred to going to "The Country" as going "Upstate." And thus Bashevkin dedicates this poem to all of you who love this and every other country.

"You mean to say
You'll send it
To my address in the city?
I'm leaving to the "Country" soon
So that *vould* be a pity!"

"Don't send it to the city
To the Country, I'll soon go"
(A place I'm sure, the motor clerk
Just simply did not know.)

The clerk indeed
Looked quite confused,
"Which Country tell me please?
A New York issued license
Will not work overseas!

"You must mean, "To *A* Country
What Country would that be?"
The fellow looked at her
And scoffed
"The Country? Liberty!"

"There is no Country, Liberty!
No Country and no State!
I'll show you in my atlas
To set the record straight."

"Liberty's *der* Country
De Country *vhere* I go!
Some *chevra* go to Ellenville
And others to Monroe!"

"Monroe?"
She asked incredulous
"Monrovia! I Hear Ya'
That's not a place in Liberty
But the Country of Liberia!"

"I'm not going to Liberia
Nor to Sierra Leone
I'm going to "The Country"
And the bungalow I own!"

Shawna was frustrated
"What Country Does that Bee?
Mister, say the Country's name
And don't say Liberty!"

The "COUNTRY *IZ
DE* COUNTRY!"
There's nothing to debate!
I think by the *moderna*
They may call it UPSTATE!"

"Just give me the address,"
She sighed,
"To your Country
I'll send it

I'm not sure where
Your Country is
But let's finish this
Let's end it!

You'll get the license
In eight weeks
Please check your daily mail
And do not drive without it
Or you might end up in jail!"

"Eight weeks!
Is Rosh Hashana!
I cannot wait so long!
He looked so sad and worried
She sensed something was wrong!

"Rush it Shawna?
You do ask
I'll see what I can do!
For a man without a Country
I will try
To help you!"

So Shawna rushed the license
It came on the right day
To a Country
That's named Liberty

. . . Is that in USA?

Do Away with Visiting Day?

In Yated Ne'eman's
Readers Write
column there
is the annual
flurry of writers
who demand
the abolishment
of visiting day.
Bashevkin muses
a "what if?"
scenario. "What if
they indeed would
abolish visiting
day?"

I looked again
The other night
At my favorite:
"Readers Write"

But what I saw
Evoked some fright
Did I really read
That letter right?

That writer had
Something to say
He would outlaw
Visiting day

What a pain
What a shlep
The agony
Of every step!

And then I stopped
And said "Oy vey!"
I wondered what if
He got his way

I imagined a world
Without that day
As children's smiles
Fade away

I would drive up
The Garden State
They would not raise
The striped toll gate
"I'm sorry sir,
you'll have to wait"

He would point
To the exit ramp
"I'm sorry sir
No trip to camp!"

The Thruway's empty
To Harriman
Except some *goyishe*
Pick-up van

Imagine on
Route 17
No cars, no litter
Only green
And cars with dogs
That look so mean

No pointing at
Some heimishe car
And knowing that
They came from far

170

No guessing where
They plan to go
Liberty?
Perhaps Monroe?

Kids standing at
The iron gate
All they'll do
Is sit and wait

No brothers, sisters
Maidels, *yingels*
No water bottles
Cans of Pringles
No envelopes
With tens and singles

Empty shops on 42
No pizza lines
And just a few
Who wait alone
Without the crowd
'Cause visiting
Was not allowed

No tales of fun
And color war
And songs
And skits
And camping lore

No cough drops
For hoarsened throats
No counselors
Handing *mitzvah* notes

No dirty nails
For Mom to scrub
No charts with names
For Cocoa Club

"Just wait" he wrote
"Just two more weeks
I won't shlep up
My car, it squeaks"
I am not sure
For whom he speaks

For me I know
10 cups caffeine
And hours on the 17
And endless waits
At the canteen
And traffic in
And out of town
And backseat noise
That I can't drown
That never seems
To quiet down

Cannot offset
The smiles greeted
And filling canteen cards
Depleted

And hearing tales
Of songs and skits
And nursing cuts
Mosquito's bits

And seeing names
On honor rolls
And hearing 'bout
Home runs and goals

And sharing moments
At the place
Where my kid won
His relay race

No pigtails flying
"Mommy, look!
Here's my camp's
Delicious cook!"

Who whispers softly
And discreet
"Your *shayfeleh*…
She doesn't eat!"

And hearing what
She learned in '*shayur*'
And she's the best
Machanayim player

"Totty, Mommy
Whadya buy us?
Totty! I learned
Most *Mishnayos*!"

So, as for me
I'll sit all day
For those few moments
That I stay

To bring a smile
To their lips
And cheer the counselors
With some tips

But soon the point
Will just be moot
As busses will
Reverse their route

And city bound
Will be our jewels
Ready for
Prospective schools

And then I'll read
Someone will say
Let's abolish
PTA!

It's Worth the Trip

It's time to pack up in your car
If you're a city man
And strap the city day camp kids
Inside your mini van

And make sure that you get them nosh
And get brand new CDs
For a trip up to the country
The land of grass and trees

Because, my friends, it's happening
Like summers that have passed
The seven hours in the car
You say will go by fast

For they're going up to visit
Their older sis and bro'
And how you make it back and forth
Only God does know

Do you shlep across the George
Or take the Tappan Zee?
Palisades or Thruway?
One thing I guarantee

That *schlepping* up
To see the kids
And show them that you care
Is worth the trip
No matter how
You managed to get there

*Visiting Day can
be harrowing for
parents who have
to travel to the
Mountains but as
always, it's worth
the trip!*

Some, they take the 42
Or some road in between
But most of us
Will suffer while
We sit on 17

But think about the smiles
When *pekelach* we bring
And when they show
The arts and crafts
And sing the songs they sing

And though their siblings
May be bored
And empty the canteen
And though you dread
Returning home
On car-packed 17

The trip up to the country
And then five hours back
And thinking that
In just a week
The kids begin to pack

I say it's still all worth it
With traffic so obscene
In hot and sticky traffic jams
And ten cups of caffeine

To *shlep* up to the country
Each *shtupped* like a sardine
To show the ones
You sent to camp
How much they really mean

The 50 Year War

Get ready for battle
Get ready to score
For fifty years going
They've been waging a War

In the mountains
The cities
Ferndale, Liberty
From Woodbourne to Stroudsburg
To Lake Chodekee

In the cities and boroughs
They all waged the war
And if it subsided
They still wanted more

The children all wait
In anticipation
While secretly sides
Evolve in formation

And suddenly happenings
That seem sort of strange
Secretly the Head Staff
Had planned to arrange

Like helicopters landing
Or milk that is blue
Or someone's gone missing
For a day, even two!

And then all the fear
the great consternation
Becomes soon a reason
For kids' celebration

A War is declared
And generals picked
Each one, to their team
Victory, they predict

And they discuss strategy
With the best of their team
To best teach some *mussar*
Through their chosen theme

'Tween fire and water
Malchus and *Kehuna*
Poor men or rich men
Bitachon, Emunah

Aish versus *Mayim*
Or Moon versus Sun
Shamayim and *Oretz*
Rabim versus One

By now this great war
that we all once knew
was not only thematic
but between Red and Blue

And of course, through the years
New colors we have seen
Like Yellow, Orange, Purple, too
And sometimes Team of Green

With races and plays
And banners
And song
And working together
With friends
All night long

And of course the grand plays
And of course the grand sing
And not making a sound
And not whispering

And sore throats and screaming
And *bentshing* insane
And counting a point
for each yelled *Amein*

The red shirts
And blue shirts
And stickers and labels
And cheering and screaming
And banging on tables

With *shmuzen* 'bout *achdus*
And clean competition
And sportsmanship, sharing
With your opposition

And then came the finale
We all stood on the floor
And the *heilege* judges
Would read out the score

They dragged it
Real slowly
While we all would sweat
And then came the scene
I'll never forget

Like kings stood the generals
Who they did anoint
And the loser, of course
Was just by a point
And suddenly chaos
Broke out in the joint

And hugging and cheering
And confetti flying
And half of bunk Aleph
Is sitting and crying

And now that my grandkids
Are going to camp
And half of them will have
Some eyes that are damp

But know, my dear children,
That all of those tears
Were some of your *Zaidy's*
Happiest years

Because what is a summer?
It would be such a bore
Without the excitement
Of the great
COLOR WAR!

Camping Out

*S*halom to our vacation homes
Our camps and bungalows
We'll miss you through the winter chills
The rains and all the snows

And all the little *kinderlach*
Soon they go *haBayta*
Good bye Aguda and Bnos
Camp Achim and Bei Kyta

Good bye, my friends
At Magen Av
Good bye my friends at Belz
Good bye to friends at Kol Torah
Where they return to Telz

Arugas Habosem and Boyan
Memories will not be gone
Toras Chaim, Camp Tashbar
Soon it shall be left so far

On winding roads
In winter's wake
If not for summer
We'd forsake
The hills, green grass
The tranquil lake
All for granted, we may take

And what we felt
And what we've seen
Are somewhere lost on 17

Leaving the Mountains, the camps and the bungalows is almost as difficult as a journey into exile. It is funny how a couple of weeks of vacation can make indelible marks on a person's life and social strata.

What for some
Would summer be
Without Stolin on Chodekee?
I think not far from Poughkeepsie
(The former home of CTV)

Which Aguda is the best
Ferndale, Toronto or Midwest?

Morris, Ohr Shraga
Mesivta Rayim
Don't forget
Adas Yereim
Staffed by
Dedicated rabbeim

Kesser, Regesh, Mah Navu
Dora Golding, Romimu
Each one
Has a place for you

Packing, *shlepping*
Clothes and *seforim*
From Camp Heller
And Na'arim
Of course
Let's not forget Camp Horim

Crafts and prizes
Loads of junk
Stuffed into the duffel, trunk
With circus memories
From Camp Munk

Yes, indeed
We've brought them home
Through Nageela
And Boy's Zone

And don't forget
Kiruv, indeed
The warriors
on Project SEED

Memories
We all will take
From Govoah,
Silver Lake

Toras Chessed, Camp Achim
Slowly lights are going dim
Pools are drained
And no more swim
Cobwebs forming
In the gym
Bereft of
Jumping *bochurim*

Camps in Moscow
And Kiev
Satmar, Sqver
Kavunas Halev

Regesh, Pupa and Boyan
Soon they'll leave
And all be gone

The *maidelach*
Will shed a tear
For all the fun
They had up here
Promises of "back next year"

Fayga, Shalva, Ranninu
Chedva, Shira
Machanenu

Sternberg, Deena
And Girl's Zone
To each a camp
Their very own

Fayga, Gila
They did come
Leaving Tubby
Looking glum
Waving bye
Chayil Miriam

Of course for those
Of noble task
At Simcha
Ohel, and Camp HASC
In Hashem's sunlight
They will bask
Responding, "yes" to every task

And so the children say good-by
To fresh air fun
And clear blue sky
To leave this place
They all ask, "why"
Teardrops form
As some do cry

But you promise
Wipe the tear
And say, "We will
Come back next year!"

Except the bungalow
On some green hill
Will not be one named Catskill
For bungalows on hills we own
Will be on mountains
Like Meron,
Har Carmel or Mount Chermon

For Moshiach's donkey
Shall be seen

Sometime soon
. . . on 17

A New Day Dawns

*T*he sun has set on summer's fun
The trunks are all unpacked
They start to breed the spider's webs
In darkness where they're stacked

And now the mode to transport stuff
Bags with padded straps
Some with names, status proclaims
And some quite plain, perhaps

And they're not filled with swimwear
Or globs of suntan lotion
Some filled with tears, some with fears
And lots of raw emotion

'Cause in those bags we send to school
Are books so filled for learning
And hopes for all the *kinderlach*
That they fulfill our yearning

For them to use the tools inside
Of backpacks and their souls
To meet the hope we set for them
And go beyond those goals

And so you will wave goodbye
And send them off to *cheder*
And with a teardrop in your eye
You'll say, "I'll see you later"

And when the summer ends, one can always wait till the next one to come...

181

For later that you'll see them
You say a silent prayer
That sometime in the future
They'll be exactly where

Your dreams and aspirations
Have aimed for them to go
According to their *kochos*
Each *al pi darko*

And as the sun has set on fun
And school is in their eyes
Even though,
One sun has set

. . . Another will soon rise

Educational Ideas

Back To School

*T*he sounds of camp have faded
They're now a memory
The kids came home
Unpacked the trunks
And left us with laundry

The clothes are washed
But they're too small
They all grew, as a rule
So now it's time for shopping
As the kids go back to school!

New shirts and coats
And uniforms
Waiting hours in line
Assuring every nervous child
All will be just fine

Pens and paper
Markers, too
Marble notebooks
For Grade One
And it's my job
To convince them all
It's gonna be such fun!

But actually
In each one's mind
School can be just great
With just the proper attitude
How to anticipate

Every year, we go through the same "Back to School" rituals. Indeed, the excitement and trepidation fades. Oh! But if, we were able to capture it for eternity.

If each day that your kid comes home
He's greeted with a **WOW**!
"You must have learned so much today
You're really smart by now!"

The enthusiasm of that start
Must carry on each day
"What happened? How did things go?"
Whether schoolwork or at play
With loving hugs
Find out what bugs
Your child, every day

Address those needs quite cautiously
Always lend an ear
Listen 'bout the silly stuff
And show them that you care

It's not about how much they learned
Just let them be their best
Let them know it's about them
And not about the test
Of course, there's work
They all must do
I mean not to deride
If they see that you care for them
And look at them with pride

Then kids will love
The school you choose
Because they know, that you care
You've instilled a spirit of
Excitement in the air

As leaves fall
With winter's chill
And things become mundane
Monotony of ritual
Can drive some folks insane

Menorahs made from bottle caps
And *dreidel* songs a dozen
Keep the smiles on their face
Enthusiasm buzzin'

The winter snow is melting
You stow away galoshes
Purim *shpiels* and *Hagados*
And kids with fifty *kashes*

Don't forget that each one counts
Appreciate the Rebbe
"Wow, what a great project you made!"
Though it may look quite *nebby*…

Enthusiasm is the key
To help our children thrive
For school is really
Where they'll bloom
Not merely just survive

So as they board that yellow bus
Make sure you remember
Each day, keep up
That fresh approach
As if it were September!

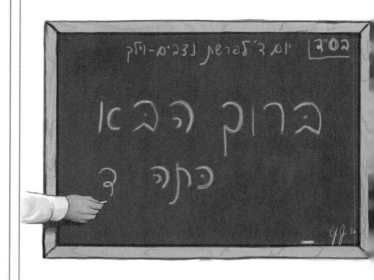

*A*lone he sits and heads the class
Of twenty five or more
And then they pushed another few
Inside his classroom door

And charge him with a mission to
Mold these eager minds
Of different scopes, abilities
And other sorts and kinds

And mend the broken,
Bolster meek
And cater to the bright
And answer to their every need
No matter day or night

On of the least appreciated professions that we have is the educator. Bashevkin muses in an ode to those who serve the future of their people with selfless devotion and sacrifice.

Rejoice at their Bar Mitzvas
And share their joy and pains
No matter who
May leave their life
The Rebbe still remains

And Morah's there
For all the girls
Whose parents'
may not "get it"

To know just when
She should protest
And when she should
Forget it
The job indeed is treacherous

Exactly when to hold 'em
And when the need
Indeed appears
Exactly when to scold 'em

Each child has his history
Which motivates his future
While teachers guide
And must decide
What to sew and suture

And all this done
For meager pay
And checks
So often late

Divine reward
Is the accord
That they anticipate

So as you pack
The kids to camp
And send them off
With smiles
And as you shop
For all their stuff
And push carts
Down the aisles

Remember that
There is one thing
That no money can buy

For all the work
That teachers do
Is sure in short supply

So take the time
Before the start
Of all your summer plans
And write a note
And here's a quote

"Thank you!
From your fans!"

*H*onorable *mentchen*
At a convention
Did I mention
With one intention

To grow
To learn
To teach
To yearn

To ensure that
The young ones learn
When to be gentle
When to be stern

Converse with those
Who duly chose
A lifetime pledge
A child grows
And *mesorah*
Believes and knows

To bask and hear
From yesteryear
Unbroken chains
Direction clear
They come again
Year after year

To hear, to bask
To seek, to ask
Because they care
To speak, to share
Year after year

From all across
The fruited plain
How to impart
How to explain

So children shall
Always remain
Their heritage
They will sustain

As never old
Never arcane
Always new
Never mundane

The challenge met
Head on each day
With meek support
And little pay

Few bonuses
No corporate checks
And bailout funds
No one expects

Bashevkin is not often invited as Poet Laureate to the Torah U'Mesorah Convention, but his one visit there and greeting scores of Rabbeim and teachers who give their lives to teach Torah inspired him to write these lines.

Torah Umesorah
תורה ומסורה

The National Society
for Hebrew Day Schools

And yet they come
Back each day
To teach our children
Our way
How to live
To learn
To play
Each and every
Single day

And once a year
A respite for
Those who accept
Their holy chore

To nurture those
They all adore
And they come back
To look for more
To teach our hopes,
The future *dor*

The sweetness of
Our holy Torah

Thank you
Torah Umesorah

In the Doldrums

*A*nd so they read Bashevkin's lines
That praised the teaching staff
And with a smirk upon their face
They all let out a laugh

"They just write about teachers
They think the rest are bums
And here we sit
And stand for it
Us in all the doldrums

"What about the little guy
Who's faltering in debt
He gets no praise
Of course a raise
Is something he won't get

"What about the mailmen
Who bring us all the mail
No snow days off
No cold or cough
Will ever let him fail

"And what about the plumber
Who comes in mid the night
To unclog drains
And floods from rains
Or make the toilet right

Bashevkin often praises teachers and educators, leaving him open to criticisms from those in other professions that serve so many while struggling to put bread on their table.
One letter he received from a disgruntled layman rightfully complained about the difficulties of other professions, and that they, too, should be praised. It was signed, "In The Doldrums."

"And why not the accountant
Who gets your taxes done
Those April weeks
Some break he seeks
For your K-401

"Let's hear it for the doctor
Who cares for all your kids
The HMO
Which pays so slow
And extras it forbids

"The executive director
Who tries to run the school
Collects tuition
No recognition
They treat him like a fool

"The seforim salesman sits all day
Inside his *seforim* store
They come take looks
Inside some books
And they walk out the door

"What about the actuary
Who all day crunches numbers
Insurance rate
He will debate
All day until he slumbers

"Let's hear it for the butcher
All day dead meat he handles
Don't ask me why
But he's the guy
Who's blamed for all the scandals

"The *shaitel macher* sits all day
While plastic hair she snips
Her clients *shmooze*
The latest news
And hardly leave her tips

"What about the drummer
Who helps us dance and sing
He clops all night
Oft out of sight
And soon hears not a thing

"Let's write about yeshiva cooks
Who toil in the heat
They make goulash
The boys eat nosh
'Cause they don't like this meat

"And what about the publisher
Who stays up Tuesday night
And what he wrote
They get his goat
Just read the "Readers Write"

"Photographers sweat every night
With all the shots they took
But there's no praise
When he portrays
If they don't like the way they look

"And what about the carpenter
Who clops away each day
But that's not right
This wood's too light
I do not want to pay

So I guess you "in the doldrums"
I missed some praise for you
You work so hard
But you feel scarred
For everything you do

"But here's this ol' Bashevkin
Who praises Reb and Morah
You want a raise
If not, some praise
Sorry but . . .

Nothing comes to teaching Torah

Signs of the Times

Who Are You?

In March of 2008, the Lakewood Jewish community was shocked to learn that one of its newer members, a man who called himself Natan Levi, was indeed not a "frum" man, but rather a Christian, and a fugitive from the FBI, whose real name was Ted Larry Floyd. He and his wife had been living in the Forest Park area of Lakewood, NJ for a few years, sent their children to a Yeshiva, davened three times a day, but they were not even Jewish! Bashevkin looked at the scene philosophically, "Are we, ourselves, always who we say we are?"

*T*his is the Tale
of Ted Larry Floyd
A Jewish life
He once enjoyed

All *treif*, he said
He would avoid
Which got the FBI
Annoyed

Straight from Kansas
On the lam
Decided to
Commit a sham
Not your typical
Lakewood scam

You see, things in Kansas
Got hot and heavy
Floyd changed his name
to Natan Levi

And where can one go
For support?
For a *tzorah*
Of any sort

He partnered in Torah
And started to learn
To the town of Lakewood
He'd sojourn

Got a *chavrusa*
for first *seder*
Got his kids
into some *cheder*

Had no problem
Getting them in
To turn them down
Would be a sin!

In a Torah
Wrote an *Ois*
(*Mevushal* for his
Shabbos kois!)

No one thought
Too much of that
So long as he
Wore his black hat!

But Purim, it came
Crashing down
The FBI
They came to town

And who'd believe
On Purim too
Another
V'Nehapoch hu!

So what's the point
For me and you
Not just a tale
'Bout a fake Jew

I think that there's more
Than meets the eye
More than questions
How and why

It's not
About Larrys
It's not about Teds
It's not about anyone
Running from Feds

The question in which
Everyone delves
Are we always
Ourselves?

It's nice to ask
Yes. You and me
Are we whom
We ought to be?

Or, my friend
May I just ask
Do we also
Wear a mask?

Yes

The question that
We hope avoid

Are WE ever
Teddy Floyd?

The Campaign

Well, my friends
The race is on
And madness
Starts to reign

They drool
And fight
For every vote
Obama and McCain

Like Crazy Ed
The claims
They make
Are none short
Of insane!

They'll scream
And shout
Bicker and whine
There'll be all sorts
Of wailin'

Accusations
Double talk
Between
Biden and Palin

Those tiny states
With no people
And no one seems to care
Will soon be combed
For sordid tales
Alaska, Delaware

"The man, he's
Inexperienced
He cannot lead the States"
"The man's too old to be
the Chief
What awful running mates!"

The election process in the United States is a wonderful side show that unfortunately takes center stage. But whether it is the election of 2008, or an election that takes place years in the future, our perspective must embody the belief that "laiv melachim v'sarim" are in the Hands of the Almighty.

199

"The woman's
Inexperienced
She can't be a beat away"

"The Senator
He's too old school
And has too much to say!"

But for all the
Speeches spoken
And all the
Lectures preached

Of how to fix
What's broken
Repair foundations
Breached

We know it
Means so little
Whoever wins
This race

When our
World's so brittle
With all the
Fears we face
So let's not
Turn to pages
Predictions
That depress

Instead our hopes
And fears relieve
In *tefilla*
We express
That no matter
Who will win this
Accept and
Not condemn

For *Leiv Melachim*
V'sarim
Is all
B'Yad Hashem

And when the winner
Does emerge

We must say it
　　　　Once again…

For *Leiv Melachim*
V'sarim
Is all … *b'Yad Hashem*

Election Reflection

*I*magine that my name was picked
They chose me now to run
What an opportunity!
It would be loads of fun!

I'd get to make my speeches
And get to press the flesh
And promise that the government
I'd reform and refresh

I'd make a million promises
With hopes to keep each one
Oh, the things I'd love to do
If only I could run

I'd promise chickens for each pot
Like politicos of old
In fact I'd promise that the pot
Would be filled up with gold

I'd promise to cut taxes
Yet, give out loads of cash
Then say, "The size of government
I'll guarantee to slash!"

I'd get rid of the IRS
Perhaps the DMV
And for all of your permits
I'd cancel every fee!

Every year the politicians stump with all sorts of promises. They are repeated year after year, and broken as often as they are repeated. Bashevkin muses, as to what would happen if he were to run for higher office.

I'd open up the government
With full transparency
Oh, what a country you would have
If you'd just elect me!

I'd bring us all together
In perfect harmony
There would be no divisions
From sea to shining sea!

And as I was delivering
This forceful speech of mine
An older fellow with grey hair
Yelled something out of line

"Mister, hold your rhetoric!
And all the things you say
'Cause it is just impossible
To do those things your way"

And so I thus
Confronted him
And shouted
"Sir! Why not?
I know I will
Accomplish them
With all the clout
I got!"

He laughed and said
"Impossible!
You cannot do them all!
There is a simple reason
You cannot overhaul

"For you simply just cannot
    improve
On all that has been done
Or fix all that has been fixed
By everyone who's run!

"'Cause all the things
You said you'll do
Surely have
Been done!

"By every politician
Who promised . . .

And then won!"

Ois'geklunked

And so my President
Has been real nice
To give us cash
Not once, but twice

When cash ran out
Some time before
He said, We'll print
A billion more!"

But now that cash
Is gone, my friend
As "Cash for Clunk"
Came to an end

And so, like Bush
It got the ax
(I'm not sure why…
Just make a tax!)

And then I thought
Just cars that clunk?
Let's get rid
Of much more junk!

Let's rid the
Speaker of the House
Or Hillary
Perhaps her spouse!

I'm sure that with
Her friend Barack
She'd put him on
The chopping block!

How much cash
You think shall do
To rid us of
Those ill-famed two?

What about
The IRS?
That old clunker
Is a mess

Imagine! Throw it
In the trash!
And get a
Pocketful of cash!

I wish he'd do
That clunker bluff
And let me trade
More broken stuff
Much of which
I've had enough

Or my old couch
That popped a spring
I'd love some cash
For that worn thing

The concept of the American government taking over car companies and banks, taking back old cars to buy you new ones is reminiscent of a failed system that we once fought mightily. It sounds wonderful now, but who knows what it may lead to?

A thousand bucks
Would be just fine
I'd get a couch
That could recline

Or take my fridge
Can't close the door
The fridge was made
In sixty-four

I can't unscrew
The inside light
(Can't open it
on Friday night!)
The freezer does not
Work quite right

Doesn't freeze
It's often hot
Mr. Prez
Some cash you got?

Or take my old
Gas range and stove
Takes more fuel
Than car I drove!

Why just cars
You say to buy?
I think I know
The reason why
For cars you were
Such a nice guy

And why you gave
Much cash for them
'Cause after all
You own GM!

And so perhaps
Just grab GE®
And send a
Microwave to me!

And then take over
Frigidaire®
And send a new one
Over here

And why not bail out
IBM ®
I surely could use
One of them

Just print those bucks
You say to spend
Or tax them from
My richer friend

I think, I feel
We have a trend
America is
On the mend

Heroes on the Moon

*I*t's been already 40 years
Remember where you *wuz*?
When three brave men ascended Earth
Neil and Mike and Buzz

Forty years has long since past
But it's like yesterday
The world was in disharmony
Chaos and disarray

It seems like it's been centuries
Since 1968
The USA
In disarray
The country we thought great

They had shot the great Black leader
And Bobby was gunned down
And Abbie and the other six
Ruled Chicago Town

And Hubert did not make it
For Nixon was "the one"
And 1969 arrived
Our country all but gone

From 'Nam just came the body bags
And riots swept the slums
And colleges were nothing but
A breeding place for bums

Forty years have passed since the world stood mesmerized as Man stepped foot on the moon. They were hailed as heroes by all the world's citizens. Bashevkin muses, "Where are this generation's heroes?"

And then three men ascended
Mike and Buzz and Neil
And finally a sense of pride
Was all that we could feel

We suddenly had heroes
We had the right to brag
For we had beat the Communists
To plant the lunar flag

And now four decades later
A footprint does remain
And it looks down
At Mother Earth
A world again insane

A world now with few heroes
Who adulate just drugs
No morals or sincerity
Just apathy and shrugs

Where are the brave of USA?
We laud those who make jokes
And glorify those decadent
Whose values are a hoax

And soon we will forget them
And Walter has no news
A generation wandering
Which lives just to amuse

And heroes found among us
Yes sad, but very few
Like Sully and his passengers
And his entire crew

But they will be forgotten
In this world now gone insane
And no one will
Remember names
Like Dole, Bush, and McCain

And soldiers are pariahs
Police are all suspect
Tables turned, and criminals
Earn undue respect

And those who hit
Their homeruns
Just sign their names for cash
No longer visit sick kids
Just golden teeth they flash

And kids no longer wonder
Where did the US go
There's no more Ronald Reagan
And no more Joltin' Joe

Respected politicians
Are scandalized each day
They don't learn from sins of past
A new crime found each day

Indeed at 9/11
Some thirty-odd years later
You did emerge
From moon-walked dirt
To fill another crater

Those heroes soon forgotten
Lungs filled with soot and silt
And the crater that they died for
Still remains unbuilt

Goodbye, our US heroes
They left you on the moon
I doubt that you
Will land back home
At least for some time soon

I hope we find more heroes
The US needs some soon
Perhaps the only heroes left
Are footprints on the moon

To the Call!

A moment's notice
Then the shake
A Caribbean
Island quake

A magnitude
They'd never seen
In a place
We've never been

Why would we notice?
Why would we care?
Why would anyone
Go there?

I sit and ponder
And I muse
What has Haiti
With the Jews?

And yet they come
To aid, to feed
A nation different
Yes, indeed
No questions asked
With lightning speed

Magen David, IDF
Fly to a world
Destroyed, bereft

Shomrim, Zaka
Do not wince
Fly to help in
Port-au-Prince

And who is there
Along their side
Yidden coming
Far and wide

Teams of all types
Every squad
Hatzolah, Chaveirim
And Chabad
Ask and they
Just give the nod

And once again
The world acts dumb
Forgets the children
Of Avraham

They're there no matte
Who's in pain
To help and help
And help again

And by the way
I'd like to know
Where's Hamas
And PLO?

In January of 2009, a devastating earthquake struck Haiti. Thousands perished in the chaos under the rubble of collapsed buildings and infrastructure. Many nations sent money but Israel sent aid. Soldiers, field hospitals, extraction experts, and their dogs. Once again, the world took no notice. But we did.

No Place Like Home

In the Spring of 2009, veteran White House reporter, Helen Thomas, a longtime Palestinian supporter, was asked by Rabbi David Nesenoff at the White House's Jewish Heritage Celebration, "Any comments on Israel?" Her response? "They should get the Hell out of Palestine! Remember, these people are occupied, and it's their land, not German and not Polish." Nesenoff followed up, "So where should they go?" Thomas responded, "They should go home." Nesenoff asked, "Where is home?" Thomas smugly replied, "Poland and Germany."

Bashevkin looks for a home for Israel.

*O*h Helen! Oh Helen!
Oh where shall I go?
You say to go home
But where? You don't know!

Oh Helen! Oh Helen!
Oh, where is my home
Is it Babylonia?
Maybe it's Rome?

Oh Helen! Oh Helen!
They sent me away
From the home that I loved
And I now live today

So maybe to Greece
And the great Parthenon
Where if we kept *Shabbos*
They said we were gone

Oh Helen! Oh Helen!
I ask you again
Where is my home
Perhaps it is Spain?

Oh Helen! Oh Helen!
It's Spain do you say?
All warm and toasty
On the *auto-de-fe*!

Perhaps back to France
Ah, the French Riviera!
Where they burned our *Talmud*
And killed us in terror

And centuries later
Your friends are all waiting
'Cause France is now Arab
So viciously hating

Did I hear you say Poland?
Is that our homeland?
Where neighbors would beat us
With sticks in their hand

And neighbors would greet us
And their children too
"Go back to Palestine
You dirty Jew"

Oh Helen! Oh Helen!
With great accolades
Says go back to Europe
And join the Crusades

Perhaps you mean Russia
The land of the Czars
Where libels and beatings
Have still left us scars

Oh! Perhaps you mean Stalin
To Communist rule
Where Jews were the scapegoat
For everyone cruel

The Reds they would jail us
The Whites would play dumb
Whenever they wanted
They'd make a pogrom

To the Pale shall you send us?
Or Siberian ice?
Is that our home
Mrs. Thomas, so nice?

Did I hear you say Germany?
Are you out of your mind?
No Jew should step foot there
The scourge of mankind

Perhaps *you* should move there
When you retire
It's cozy in Auschwitz
They'll leave on the fire

Romania, England
Hungary, Brazil
Oh! The places to go
Where they're ready to kill
Oh Helen! Oh Helen!

Where is my home?
You think it's the land
Where the buffalo roam?

Is home a sweet country
Where thousands are lost
To dream of a dream
Whatever the cost?

And lose their identity
Their faith and their links
That is not home
It's great, but it stinks

I've heard some
Strange comments
But this is the worst
From that crazy old lady
From the papers of Hearst

You sit and you spew
From your front White House seat
Your Jew hatred open
No longer discreet

I'll go back home, Helen
To the land I know is mine
A land that we call Israel
And you call Palestine
I will not say this softly
It's surely worth a shout
"But we will *not* leave Palestine
No, we won't get out!"

For we need to go nowhere
We are home, we are here
And you, Mrs. Thomas,
Where *you* go, we don't care

Where we may find you?
I really don't know
Wearing a burqa
On some video?

Goodbye and good riddance
We won't "see you later"
Unless your the spokesman
For your friends at Al-Qaeda

The Leak

On April 20, 2010, an oil well in the Gulf of Mexico, that had just been drilled by British Petroleum, exploded into a huge fireball. The damaged platform sank and a broken pipe leaked oil into the Gulf for more than 80 days. Millions of gallons of oil escaped from the well and gushed to the surface.

After many months and failed attempts, it seems that the leaking pipe has finally been capped. Bashevkin muses about lessons that he learned from the disaster.

*I*t's plentiful
And now it's free
Get oil now
Straight from BP!

It's not as simple
As it seems
Just come on down
To New Orleans

And bring some pitchers
For black gold
Before it's harvested
And sold

Yes, my friends
The Gulf is goo
With oil there
For me and you

And for the fish
Of that great sea
Thanks to the guys
Who run BP

They have no *mazel*
And no *glick*
To try to stop
The oil slick

Put on a dome
Poured in cement
But spewing out
The oil went

And now the Prez
He has banned
All oil that
Comes not from sand

Why do the Arabs
Have the luck
They have no seas
To spew their muck

Their oil comes
From under sands
No worries when
On dirt it lands

But more than that
I'd like to ponder
Of issues that
Are way
Down yonder

That as the oil
Is still leaking
May I compare it
To our speaking

For once it's out
It won't stop gushing
Leaving people
Shamed and blushing

And no matter what
The deed is done
The oil leak
Has just begun

A dome won't stop it
Nor cement
And that is surely
Not what you meant
When words that leaked
From you were sent

So perhaps the leak
May be a sign
Sent by
Heavenly design

To teach a lesson
To our soul
That once it leaks
You lose control

Musing On Madness

Temporal Towers of Eternity

*T*hose towers stood
Their height profound
The symbols of
The sure and sound

Of power, fame,
And fortune found
Now lie crumpled
On the ground

Their skin is peeled
Their guts exposed
As beauty writhes
In pained repose

The shimmer of
A sheen like new
Ashen now
With residue
The remnants of
Its might and wealth
Sitting in
Its humbled stealth

The first poem that Bashevkin wrote and published was penned in the emotional aftermath of 9/11. There was so much anger and angst, fear and unclarity, yet there were lessons to be garnered from the crumpled mass of steel that lay at the foundation of New York City.

Yet from the ruins
Of their might
Emerges yet
A different sight
Where all are equal
In their need
No stocks, no bonds,
No wealth, no greed

Facades of shining vanity
Melted by insanity
Can this be wrought
By our humanity?
Destruction of urbanity
Through missiles of profanity

Walls of glass have long been shattered
Metal beams like paper tattered
Power drinks have long since splattered.
Memos and their authors scattered
Nothing now has ever mattered

What can we learn from broken beams?
Where nothing is as nothing seems
Where souls ascend to missions calling
Some by rising, some by falling

The inner essence of the towers
Shines so bright in these bleak hours
When death has beckoned bold and great
A crooked finger, points their fate

Towards strangers they would soon defend
And kiss the moment with their end
Acknowledging the pure Godsend

And from the ashes does arise
A valiant ear that hears the cries
And runs toward it despite the threat
To pull, to carry, aid, abet
A new foundation has been set

What now like Phoenix does arise?
Is the response unto the cries
A new façade toward heaven soars
Piercing the celestial doors

For nothing can be built above
What now's been built by faith and love
And missiles now will never breach
The lessons that those souls did teach

The search for Osama Bin Laden has been ongoing for more than ten years. Truth be told, as Jews we are always on the lookout for the Bin Ladens who are out to harm us. The war against the West has been battled on the streets of the Holy Land for decades. To our American hosts it may be new, but to us it has been an ongoing struggle, which I am afraid will only end with the ultimate redemption.

We've *bin* waitin'
For Bin Laden
He's *bin* gone
But not forgotten

Were we thinkin'
This could happen?
If we hadn't
Bin caught nappin'
It's *bin* old news
To our brothers
Just that they're Jews
The slighted *others*

Has the war now
shifted places?
Different buildings
Different faces
Same old venom
Newfound races?

The acts we dread
A feared tomorrow
Yesterday's acts
At Sbarro

220

So will the fear
And stomachs sinking
Shake our mindset
Get us thinking
That the hatred is not pithy
Focused on the Holy City

Rather it is noted best
For anything
That smells of West
For we understood way back
Before the dastardly attack
The tiny State was just a pawn
Initial place to darken dawn
Their hatred has a larger host
Purple Mountains to the Coast
And if we'd done what we sure can
There'd have *bin* no Laden, Taliban

Rest not on
Domestic laurels
And say that these
Are not our quarrels
For in a world
With sacred ties
We all must know
Where friendship lies
For borders shall not separate
When bizarre sense
Breeds bizarre hate

Wondering Why

*A*n act of violence
Done at random
All the newscasts
Said in tandem

"They're searching
For the motivation"
Said the newsman
At the station

They are all baffled
They wonder why
The CIA and FBI

After all
He made a living
Middle class
Caring, giving

So why on earth?
There is no way
A man would shoot
Two Jews one day

Imagine that your CNN
Was skewing stories way back then
With naïve eyes that gave no clue
About the persecuted Jew

Cast a look at Bernard Shaw
Reporting news
From days of yore

On July 4, 2002, an Arab taxi driver, Hesham Mohamed Hadayet, randomly murdered two Israelis at the El Al ticket counter at the Los Angeles International Airport. One was a ticket agent and the other was Yakov Aminov, a diamond importer. Hadayet was killed during the attack by an El Al security guard.

The following is a direct quote from a CNN News Bulletin:

"Investigators methodically sifted through what they could of the life of Hadayet, trying to find a motive behind the deadly attack."

Bashevkin wonders, "When are they going to get it?"

"The Temple, today, was burned to the ground
A reason why cannot be found"

Spain in 1492
It was a crime to be a Jew
I'd love to see the newscasts then
Reporters preaching "why and when"

"Ten Jews were killed, auto-de-fe"
We don't know why,
No one could say
The motive Torquemada had
They must have done
Something real bad

. . . . and now for the Sports

Chelmenitzki came this way
And hacked 600 Jews today
Police are looking
For a reason
They're sure that it's not
Killing season

. . . . and now for the International News

Crusades today massacred Worms
The anchor reads and slightly squirms
Authorities in Rome are taken aback
What provoked the cruel attack?

.... and now for the Arts

Today, King Louis, rebuffed some arts
He burned some books, twenty-four carts
We're sure it was not really cruel
Perhaps, his palace needed fuel

Yes! Vicious hateful history
Remains to them a mystery
Why they do it no one knows

Two thousand years of random acts
Read some truth, observe the facts
Abhorring Jews is inculcated
From churches, mosques it's procreated

And yet the world thinks love and hugs
Looks dumfounded as it shrugs
Are they fools
Or are they blind?
Or are they just
Out of their mind?

The fiend who shot us in LA
Did not emerge within a day
It was not for a lack of pay
A lousy fare, a bad hair day

The rhetoric
That reeks of hate
Through his world
Did dissipate

When children's Ernie
Or their Bert
Speak tones of hatred
Taught to hurt

A Jihad on the enemy
Throw his children to the sea
They killed our god
Our blood they drink
What do you expect
Their folk to think?

Songs that sing of
Death and plunder
Why he'd shoot Jews
They all still wonder

Babies dressed
For suicide
Those pictures are
Their joy and pride

Wake up, world, and smell the grind
And understand what is behind
A millennium of lies
That taught these people to despise

So when you look for motivation
Try to think — Jihad — Salvation
And when those words are clear to you
You'll report differently
'bout me,
The Jew

A Kiss Apart

In the summer of 2002, Martin F. was standing outside a falafel shop in Jerusalem when it exploded. A trained medic, he went in and discovered the body of a young man on the floor. The young man had lost both legs below the waist, as well as an arm, but his eyes were open and focused. A few seconds passed while the two looked at each other. Knowing it was probably in vain, Martin F. decided to administer mouth-to-mouth resuscitation. After a minute or two, the young man's eyes rolled up into his head and he expired. As he walked out, Martin F. saw that a group of people had gathered, including two policemen, who wanted to know how many casualties were inside. When he responded that there was only one, Martin F. realized the young man he had just left inside was a suicide bomber.

The story's true
It came direct
From the pen of
The pathetic hero

On a fateful day
He was going his way
Then BOOM!
A personal ground zero

He came from the USA
To the Promised Land
A twist of fate
Destiny's date
At a falafel stand

A meeting that
He never planned
Heroics are hard
To understand
Yet Heaven's will
Will always land
In laps of simple
Mortal man

Marty, a medic
Peripatetic
Meandered
To get himself
A bite that morning
The bomb, you see
Human debris
Detonated
Without warning

So Marty raced
To the fateful place
His caution not
Forbearing

A medic
He was trained for this
Approaching
Without fearing

The scene that
Greeted him,
Of course,
Was nothing
Less than madness
Tables and chairs
Bodies and tears
The grim rubble
Of sadness

Charred and scorched
The stand was torched
Its patrons
Thrown asunder

Who will live?
And who will not?
If surely makes
One wonder
But Marty sped
And risked his life
And yet it was for zero

Midst shrill alarm
He ran past harm
As one to be a hero

A child gone
A mother maimed
And dozens more lay hurt
And one man looked
So awfully torn
With death he seemed to flirt

Marty, a trained EMT
Ran to save his life
Another casualty of war
Of madness and of strife

Mouth to mouth
He put his lips
And breathed his strongest breath
With prayer in heart and
Lips apart
He'd save the man from death

And then he saw
Fate had in store
A lesson not forgotten
The victim that
He chose to save
Was something
Worse than rotten
For on his waist
Remained the charred
Remnants of mass murder

For with a bomb
Packed with aplomb
His loins he chose to girder

The evil man did ebb away
While Marty coiled back
And realized that
He breathed his breath
To the mouth of the attack

His Jewish lips
Touched Arab ones
From worlds so far apart
To save a dying soul he tried
The scene won't leave his heart

The lips that touched each other
Were mutually detested
He almost saved a savage beast
With breath that he invested

But yet, who knows
What could have been
From only one small breath
For life, means hope
For change, for peace
And there is life 'til death

But 'til that day
It's sad to say
All that remains is schism
Invectives and hatred's seeds
Sown with terrorism

And though
A separate people
We'd live
With firm accord

With those so fit
To soon admit
Our land
Came from the Lord

And he and I
By chance could work
In this falafel station

Helping all together
With true cooperation
We could have shared in
Partnerships
With joy,
Perhaps embrace

In medicine
In commerce
In worlds
Where we're one race

But the evil of
The rabid voice
Set his brain on fire
And killing Jews
Their babes, and folks
Becomes the sole desire

We could have
Had a friendship
A mutual revere

Two children of
An Abraham
A patriarch
To share

And now he lay
Just blown to bits
And death lies
In his wake

And lips that could
Have touched in joy
Now cry for their mistake

228

Security in the Skies

In December of 2009, a terrorist unsuccessfully tried to detonate his explosive underwear on a flight to Detroit. He evaded security, as in deference to political correctness he was not scrutinized. Meanwhile instead of pursuing terrorists, Homeland Security seems to chase any object that may be turned into an incendiary device. Bashevkin wonders if checking baby bottles instead of scrutinizing people is the way to go.

America
I ask, pray tell
Do you think
That all is well?

On the ground
Or in the air
Will someone soon
Please start to care

First a madman
Thought to use
A place to plant
His bomb, his shoes

Now we caught
Up to his ruse
And now we all
Take off our shoes

Security
Brilliantly handles
Tons of shoes
And clogs
And sandals

The skies were safe
They then did think
Until they placed
A bomb in drink!

"Oh no!" shouted
The wise old men
Never let
Drinks on again!

Unless you buy
It past the gate
At fifty times
The normal rate!

And let those tiny
Babies cry
No bottles if
You dare to fly

We'll throw them out
Won't give them back
No Isomil
No Similac!

A bomb we will not
Let it through
No mouthwash, soda
Or shampoo

Sorry, that's what
We must do
'Cause we are here
Protecting you!

229

Please, Mister
Abdulmallab
Come right here
I'll do my job

Take off your shoes
And toss your drinks
And nothing's wrong
'Cause no one thinks
The entire
System stinks

But no, it's great
We'll fix the glitch
We'll add a rule
We'll add a hitch

What's next
To check?
What's next
To pick
To save us from
The terror *shtick*?

Perhaps
the next thing
they will botch
A bomb
That's planted
In a watch

OK!
They'll say
Off with your wrist!

(They won't look at
The terror list!)

Offend someone?
Oh! Surely not!
Suspect them in
A terror plot!

Oh No! Oh No!
Heaven forbid!
We don't care what
They've said or did!

Terrorists
They don't
Bomb planes!
Or boats or cars
Or even trains!

It's bottles!
Drinks!
And even shoes!
We have to watch
Those things
They choose!

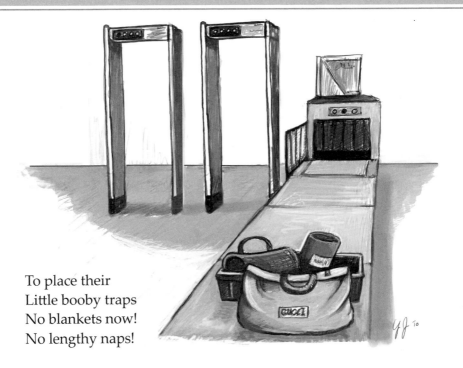

To place their
Little booby traps
No blankets now!
No lengthy naps!

And so old ladies
Alter Yidden
Maybe in your
Hat it's hidden
When will *shaitels*
Be forbidden!

A bomb a knife
Something to fear
What you look like
We don't care!
For we are kind
And we are fair
We let everyone
Fly here

We profile not
For we don't care
We love you all
We want you here
The only things
That we do fear

Bottles, shoes and …

                    Underwear

231

Gezeiras Gaza

sit and type
I'm gripped with fear
A day of reckoning
Indeed is here

Just two years back
Korbanos fell
Was it for naught
Can we now tell?

Streets are filled
Across the world
Shrieks of rage
Invectives hurled

Protest signs
And drunks who jeer
Will clutter streets
Around Times Square

Shattered glass
And broken stones
Clutter streets
In Ashkelon

And bricks are tossed
And windows blown
In Europe
Moltovs are thrown

As Ashdod's cries
Now join Sderot
And Ofakim
And Netivot

Each hammer a weapo
Screwdriver a knife
As rabid eyes
Vie for your life

Decisions made
Come back to haunt
Paid with young lives
That they now flaunt

And so my friend
With patience thin
They said, "We must
Send our boys in"

The boys, now troops
To meet the foe
Habah lehargecha
Hashkeim lehargo

In the mire they troop
In the squalor
They trudge
To root out the fiends
Who just will not budge

In January of
2009, after years
of the incessant
firing of rockets
into Israel by
Hamas, the IDF
sent troops into
the Gaza Strip in a
full-scale military
incursion.

Once again, the
world refused
to allow Israel
to defend itself,
and anti-Semitic
protests and
destruction reigned
upon Jews and
Jewish institutions
world-wide.

Faces blackened
Suppressed in green
To meet an
enemy unseen

Our hearts are pained
Our eyes are glued
A pall is cast
A somber mood
 And news will spew
Along with hate
And violence
To anticipate

Across the globe
No one is sure
Do we dare think
We are secure
How long can *golus*
Still endure?

But yet we live
In apathy
"The world will have
Some sympathy"

The children pray
Our lives move on
Sporadically
We touch upon

The pain of *toshvei*
Eretz Yisroel
Who day to day
In danger dwell

New Year's noise
Drowns out our thoughts
And stocks and bonds
And sells and boughts

Of highway jams
And silly tales
Hottest news
And latest sales

Can we focus
Stop and pray
Forget the mundane
In our day

To drown the hype
To still the noise
Distracts our focus
For the boys

Whose lives depend
On thousands here
Can we pour our hearts?
And shed a tear?

While they engage
In non-stop action
Can we find time
Without distraction?

It's hard, I know
Our minds do wander
And respite oft
Impedes our ponder
Of *tzaros* far
And way down yonder

But my friends
In USA
The fight is here
The fight's today
Mumbai and Gaza
Not far away

From broken beer glass
From the bar
Around the corner
Not so far
 Where hatred spews
Our *sonim* meet
In that same bar
Just down the street

The war in Gaza
Is our own
We are Mumbai
We're Ashkelon

They came to us
On Nine One One
They say their job
Is still not done

As far as friends
We have just One
Was here before
All this begun

The One Who will
Always be here
To Him,
A plea,
A cry,
A tear

For peace
And all
To see and hear

Yerushalayim built
Anew,

Next year

A Flotilla of Hate

This is not a musing
I'm simply not amused
I feel despondent
And depressed
And frankly
Quite abused

The human race
Quickly forgets
and soon absolves
All guilt

"Just forget
The Holocaust
Look at the State
You built"

And now all is
Forgotten
Sad to say but true
Their attitudes
And actions speak
The horrors to renew

What have they learned?
What lessons gleaned
From failed humanity?

Is sixty years
Enough to see
Revived insanity?

The world has since
Gone crazy
As monsters are adored
And victims who
Defend themselves
Are shunned, cursed
and abhorred

The world
Who brought Korea
Iran and Vietnam
The loving men
Who brought the world
Race riots and "The Bomb"

The ones who chased
The Mexicans
Mojaves and the Sioux
Will flip their lid
If it's a *Yid*
Or something like a Jew

The world who brought
Us Pol Pot
Brezhnev and
Mao Zedong
Will smirk in their
Self righteousness
When shouting,
"Israel's wrong"

And in the White House
Press room
There reigns insanity
When reporters can
Just smugly say
"Go back to Germany"

You cannot board
A phony ship
That's filled with arms of terror
And let them slip
Their dogs of war
When there's no room for error

And let the rockets
Fly to you
And never say a word
And let your own
Like Judge Goldstone
Accuse us, so absurd

Oh! Yes, my friends
This is no joke
The world has lost its mind
They'll turn their heads
From evil men
And just play dumb and blind

But any slight
Infraction done
By a single Jew
They'll rant and rave

And act depraved
Toward me
And toward you
What is the answer?
I don't know
The *golus* has its grip
Until we learn
To truly yearn
I fear that we'll just slip

And not to end
So sour
And sit and type and mope
I won't forget
Despite the threat
We have a "Rock of Hope"

And when we learn
Our lesson
Golus finally ends
A time will come
When blind and dumb
Will see and speak amends

*H*e called a summit
Just last week
Our *Prez*, Barak Hussein
He wants to stop the terrorists
To beat them at their game

And every country's wise men
with speeches they all came
All except, that single, tiny state
That they all like to blame

They said they feared the crazies
The terrorists
The kooks
They said that they'd make strategies
To stop them and their nukes

He wants to be the hero
And everyone should love him
He does not care
And does not fear
From the Holy One above him

And just as all the nations met
To say they're in control
Somewhere, a place
That's off the maps
Played a crucial role

For as they worried
'Bout the nukes
And terror's secret stash
A mountain out in Iceland Coughed
And spewed volcanic ash

In 2010, President Barrack Obama convened an international summit of world leaders during April to discuss the growing nuclear threat posed by terrorist groups and outlaw states. Israel did not send its Prime Minister, knowing all too well that he would be the focus of scrutiny. At the same time, a volcano erupted, spewing volcano ash across Europe, causing travel chaos and interruptions the likes that were not experienced since 9/11. Bashevkin muses about connections between the events.

And skies were filled
With soot and smoke
And planes sat in their tracks
While men in suits
Thought they could stop
The nuclear attacks

And said the One in Heaven
"I am in full control
Of earthquakes
Floods and tsunamis
And how they take their toll

"And those who gather
With their friends
To think that they're in charge
Should get a wakeup call to say
That they are not so large

"With all their newfound gizmos
And info they will share
Can't even stop
Bombs in underwear."

And He sits in Heaven
And He laughs
At puny men who think
That they will now control the world
As they signs their names in ink

A Putin lifts his glass so high
And sends Barack a toast
And they go home to their Parliaments
And beat their chests and boast

But all their little papers
And all the names they sign
Are all a joke
To the One who says,
"The whole wide world is Mine!

"The destiny of My chosen
Will form the world's next fate,
Not those who look at their Land
As their own real estate."

For summits
They do come and go
Like leaders of small men
And years go by, and they all pass
As we all outlive them

They sit in secret and connive
And make plans they think great
Hashem, He laughs
In Heaven high
And says, "Oh you just wait"

For one day
Avnei Elgavish
Will cover those with soot
For those who think
They own our fate
Will that day, get the boot

On Sacred Ground

In Summer of 2010, controversy brewed around plans to build an Islamic Cultural Center and mosque a few blocks away from Ground Zero. Critics decried the project as an insult to the memory of those murdered in the 9/11 attacks on the World Trade Center, and as an attempt by radicals to "triumphantly prove that they can build a mosque near the place where 3,000 Americans were killed by Muslims." Yet, liberals are pushing forward for the mosque, with cries of "Freedom of religion" on their lips. Bashevkin muses, "What type of outrage, would there be heard if similar tragic sites would be so antithetically transformed.

Imagine if we took a spot
On this great planet earth
And so abused its sanctity
Its value and its worth

Each place has some significance
Where history was made
And no one has a right to rain
On sanctity's parade

Imagine Philadelphia
Where that famous bell did peal
If they would put a minuet
And ring a call to kneel

The Library of Congress
Which holds the Constitution
Would now display the manifest
Of Russian Revolution

And Dallas' Dealy Plaza
Where Kennedy was shot
Would pay homage to Lee Harvey
Pelosi, I think not

A balcony in Memphis
Where King was shot that day
Let's make a center to learn the
Ideas of KKK

In Oklahoma City
A monument one day?
Right near the Murrah Building
To Timothy McVeigh

Freedom of religion?
I wonder if they'd wanna
Memorialize Reverend Jim Jones
In the Republic of Guyana

In fact, right near the Watergate
I hear a room they're fixin'
Filled with books and studies of
A man named Richard Nixon

I wonder if in Pakistan
Home of the Taliban
They would teach
Bible in school
Alongside the Koran

But say one word 'bout Islam
Or joke about their seer
Of tolerance and forgiveness
I'm sure we'll never hear

We've seen for petty
Small cartoons
Their vitriol was showered
And all the strong,
Now little men
Ran to their holes and cowered

But when they want
To build their mosques
All seem to kowtow to
No matter what religion
Christian, Buddist, Jew

And where they want to build
They will
And all the world will smile
They'll kill 3,000 and then say
We'll come back in a while

Indeed, it is Ground Zero
Where they want
To build a mosque
I have no English words for it
But what an open *frosk*!

Obama makes excuses
Pelosi cheers them on
Bloomberg talks so respectfully
About those who hope us gone

The memories mean nothing
The ashes are a joke
The pride that was America
Has now gone up in smoke

We'll go to Hiroshima
Say, "Sorry," to Japan
I think a global lovefest
That is our leader's plan

Perhaps we'll built a monument
Yamamoto we'll remember
And the fleet who bombed on
The seventh of December…

It's almost Rosh HaShana
And thus I think and muse
The feelings that I have for this
And what it means for Jews

For when we stand
On hallowed ground
In *yeshiva* or in *shul*
Do we act with dignity?
Does awe and respect rule?

Do we respect our sacred shrines
The places of our prayer
Do we argue, fight in them
And act as we don't care

Is our *Makom Mikdash*
A place to shed a tear?
Or just a place
To tell your friends
"Hey, let's meet over there!"

We yell and shout at liberals
And false democracy
Then we forsake
Our sacred ground
Is that hypocrisy?

Remember that with dignity
For mundane to profound
Be careful when you
Start to tread
On sacred hallowed ground

A Lighter Note

My GPS sits in a lake
The purchase
Was a big mistake
I got it with
My new "smart phone"
Which made sure
I was not alone

Among the features
That it had
They said were good
But they were bad
You see
I did not have to dial it
But soon I would revile it

They said
"Just talk"
"Just say a name"
It will dial
Just the same

The radio
Was set to sync
They said I would not
Have to think

Just name a tune
And
It will play
From MBD
To LeGabay

Just say "dial"
It would ring
Just say, "music"
It would sing
It could do most
Anything
Just say "Lakewood"
Wait and see
The GPS
To BMG

But all those toys
Worked not in tandem
Each one would
Revolt at random

The gps liked not
The phone
Each wanted
To work alone

And then we added
One more layer
A radio
And CD Player

It started on
A simple trip
And that's
When things
Began to slip

The proliferations of gadgets may be a good thing for some of us. For Bashevkin and his generation, it spelled disaster.

245

I said to it
"Please dial home"
My phone was set
To search and roam

My GPS
Picked up the sound
And started squawking
"Turn Around"

"Please," it screamed
"Make a U Turn"

A term
My radio had learned
"Turn on radio!"
It churned

It blared right on
And it did choose
For on the "eights"
The traffic news

"The George Washington"
It said to choose
My GPS
It did confuse

Cause that device
Now barked, "Turn right"
I swerved my car
That fateful night

"Bear Right"
It screamed,
"Take the Cross Bronx"
I turned my car
Despite the honks

And right in middle
Of this scourge
The phone
Began to ask,
"Call George?"

"Did you say
Call George?"
It queried
By now
I'm dizzy
Weak and wearied

So here I am
The radio blaring
On the Cross Bronx
Drivers glaring

My phone's about
To call a George
Beneath me
Is the Hudson's gorge

I gave a shout,
"It's a mistake!
I need to find
The Garden State!

"The Parkway
The Parkway!"
I cried in dismay"
The CD chimed
"Play LeGabay?"

And so, the cycle
Started to spin
The radio blared
The phone
Chimed in

The GPS was
Really grating
Over and over
"Recalculating"

To mine, or any
Other voice
Or for that matter
Any noise

And so,
All my toys
Are all now gone
The radio
Will not turn on
The phone. my friend
Will not respond

And the GPS
I bought by mistake
Sits way down in
Carasaljo's Lake

Chessed Rules

I went shopping back to Brooklyn
In my beat up Chevrolet
I thought the prices would be cheap
But, oh boy, did I pay

You see, I learned some lessons
And returned home forlorn
I tried to get a patchwork quilt
For a grandson newly born

I walked up and down the Avenue
For a store that sold a quilt
The heat was quite unbearable
I thought that I would wilt

I saw a store with baby things
I thought they'd have my gift
At a price, which would be nice
For my concern with thrift!

But there were thirteen carriages
Parked right near the door
I'm not including seven
That were inside the store

And some, they were not empty
One had a crying tot
I looked again, and saw no mom
Was I crazy or just hot?

The Borough of Park in Brooklyn, commonly referred to as Boro Park often gets a bad rap for pushy customers, indifferent salespeople, and rude citizens. However, though everyone is busy tending to the mundane needs of daily life, when even a minor crisis occurs, they spring into action with uncomparable kindness and benevolence.

This is an ode to the people of Boro Park where kindness so often rules.

I made my way inside the store
And called out for the Mom
I think she walked right past me
With an air of cool aplomb

I slowly sauntered to a case
And saw something, quite nice
But they looked at me curiously
When I asked, "What is the price?"

It seems that in that fancy store
They will take you to task
If you're on a budget
Or you just decide to ask

I thought they'd want
To make a sale
Not keep the quilt and horde it
They must have thought
"You ask the price?
Then, you simply
Can't afford it!"

So I walked out
In quite a huff
I promise, I'm not lying
The kid I saw
When I came in
Was still outside
And crying!

I looked inside the store and yelled
"Whose kid is out there yelling?"
She looked at me, I saw the eyes
The apathy was telling

"One minute! I'll be getting him
My pocketbook's a mess
I have to find my Platinum Card
American Express!"

I quickly ran back to my car
To just end this excursion
Unfortunately, I would soon have
An unpleasant diversion

I could not open my car door
No, it was not stuck
Sidled up to it, there was
An eighteen-wheeler truck!

And then I saw the driver
He looked like one of "us"
I ask nicely,
"Please move your rig"
I was sure he wouldn't fuss

I don't know what got into him
Perhaps it's what he ate
"I do not feel like moving now!
My friend, you'll have to wait!"

He must have been real busy
(Perhaps a business call?)
'Cause he just did
Not even care
About my car at all

He ran inside a pizza shop
I waited there in the heat
He doubled parked his *groise* truck
And got something to eat!

I now used the King's English
"Can you, please move the truck"
I even asked by saying "please"
But I was out of luck

The fellow just ignored me
Cared not for my sweet pleas
"*Dats* very nice,
I'll have a slice
And add some extra cheese"

Dejected, I now left the store
And figured I'd just wait
But greeting me
Was something else
I did not anticipate

For there it was, right by my d
My tire had gone flat
And in the midst
Of all my grief
I did not think of that!

Here I was, just sweltering
Beside a giant truck
How will I get out of here?
Am I forever stuck?

And suddenly
The whole world changed
The fellow ran to me

"You have a flat?
No problem, that!
I'll fix it
One, two, three!"

It was the driver of the truck!
He radioed his friend
Soon they came
With flashing lights
My tire they would mend!

And then again to my surprise
From the snooty baby store
They came with water bottles
Perhaps, three or maybe four

"Take a drink, cool off in my car
I'll turn on the AC
I know gas is expensive
But it is mitzvah for me!"

I could not believe my eyes
It was her Ms. American Express!
"My husband,
He can drive you home
We have a GPS!"

"I know you come
From out-of-town
Those strollers bothered you
But here we're always ready
To help another Jew"

We may clutter the sidewalks
Or, maybe push in line
But, when we see
A Yid in need
He is like "one of mine"

And in no time the tire's fixed
And I'm cooling in a car
Sitting here
While people *shvitzed*
For a stranger
Come from afar

Quietly I realized
That chessed's
Always here
It comes from
Deep inside of Jews
You thought
Would never care

So next time
You are pushed in line
Or treated somewhat snide
Know that a loving heart
Is hidden deep inside

It's just that in the rush of life
We get carried away
But when the push comes
    to shove…
Chessed saves the day

251

Expression Session

Bashevkin asks
To spend some sessions
To discuss strange words
And strange expressions

Where they come from
I ask, "Why?"
Let's start with
the letter "I"
When used as me
It's always big
Something I just simply
"Do not dig"

Which makes no sense
Why digging land
Has what to do
With "understand"

Of course I guess the
Answer's true
We care 'bout "I'"
Not 'bout you

Not only words
But strange expressions
Have left upon me
Some strange
Impressions

"Lashon ilgim"
What they are
Still I search for
Some *mekor*

Like I would like
To know just why
Who put the butter
In a butterfly

Like when it rains
There's cats and dogs
I don't know why
Not rats and frogs

And things so clear
Are cut and dry
Don't ask me what
Or where or why

You're dry if you
Do wear a poncho
But it don't *"pas"*
If you're top honcho

What's a honcho
Don't ask me
Your climbing up
The wrong tree!

There are many interesting expressions in the English language. This muse was inspired by a book by David Feldman, author of the Imponderable Series, "Who Put the Butter in the Butterfly?"

What's a "jig"
Why is it up?
Is a "last straw"
Made for a cup?

Perhaps this column
I should nix it
Or as they say
Perhaps "deep six it"

I know some things
Do not come soon
But what my friend
Is a "blue moon"?

Do certain people
"Get your goat"
To China they take
The slow boat

Others, sure
They do not mind
They have no axe
They'd like to grind

Please explain
The simple facts
When you're upset
Why grind an axe?

A politician
Out of luck
I think they call him
A lame duck

But that expression's
Out of whack
Isn't a bad doctor
Called a "quack"?

So I'm not sure
Why ducks take blame
To call them quacks
Or call them lame

The animal
In language plays
For summer sure has
Its "dog days"

And dogs we know
They may have fleas
But a flea market?
Tell me, please!

I hope those markets
Have no bugs
And the vendors
Are not thugs

What's a thug?
Who made that word?
Combine a thief and bug?
Absurd!

Did you ever
Wonder why
Stam a *mentch*
Is called a guy?
Why are soldiers
Called "G.I."?

Don't ask me
I do not know
Ask a soldier
Who's named Joe

Here's one I know
(I will not brag)
Who let the
Cat out of the bag?

You "run amok"
When you are flustered
And second rate
Don't cut the mustard

Vos eppes mustard?
What's "amok"?
If you ask me
You're outta luck

Many people
Not too bright
They say they seek
The great "limelight"

But why a lime?
Why that fruit?
Here's another
One "to boot!"

Freebies are things
Given for free
Are heebie jeebies
Given by hee?

I surely am
No racist man
Do Latinos make things
Spic and span?

Yes! Who put the butter
In the butterfly?
Or capitalized
The letter I?
Or said things were
Easy as pie?

If you're fired
You are "sacked"
The boss read you
The "riot act"

And if he likes you
Things are fine
Then you're sitting
On "cloud nine"

How do you get
To play that role
Wouldn't touch it
With a ten foot pole

Did you ever
Even wonder
Why grabbing the "limelight"
Is "stealing thunder"

And if one speaks
Not like a *mentch*
They ask their friend
"Pardon my French"

Why not Spanish
Portugese?
Why not
"Pardon my Chinese"?

I'll never know
I won't be coarse
But does English
Need a source?

Now *Lashon Kodesh*
Even Yiddish
Every term
Must bear a *chiddush*

Now's not the time
For that *mavucha*
I'll leave it as an
Ugah
    . . . *B'lo hafucha!*

Mumbles

I think that our kids mumble
What they say, I am not sure
The words are halfway spoken
Their diction is quite poor

Language art is clearly lost
And words are mispronounced
Alas, the English language
Is reasonably trounced

When they come home from Yeshiva
They're in a hungry mood
I'm glad there's just one syllable
When they say that "I need food"

But if the questions or request
Needs some more explanation
Indeed the folks
Who live back home
Need much more concentration

When they meet their
Aunt Bessie
Who comes in from LA
She says, "The boys are really nice
But, what did they all say?"

I'm goneing to *bshmdrsh*
Gtsumstf to learn
Be there *"foreignour"*
Then I *woolritrn.*

Every Bain Hazmanin, Bashevkin's Yeshiva boys come home and seem to have lost their diction in Yeshiva. Bashevkin decided to write an Ode to Mumbles

When they are shopping
For a suit
Or need a *Yom Tov* tie
I marvel how the salesman knows
What these kids want to buy

But they don't ask
"What was that?"
They listen very hard
When they see those boys flashing
A bright green credit card

But moms and dads
Indeed must strain
To catch the mumbled word
Or just assume
"I'll clean my room"
Is what they just now heard

Of course, the English language
Is clearly not their *shprach*
When they are learning Torah
The *'gantzer tohg uhn nacht'*

Perhaps they are not to blame
I'm sure that you'll concur
When the man who was
Once President
Pronounced it "nukuler"

And in their words, nothing is real
Cause everything's like, "like"
Whatever; forget it; OK,OK
I'll *pitaway* the bike!

And when they get
A bit older
One word, does get them far
The first few words are indistinct
The last I hear is "car"

They'll soon grow up
Shidduchim come
We hope they'll be no crisis
While each one tries to find
For them
The smartest and the nicest

But every parent out there, hopes
And is constantly praying
That each one on
The *shidduch meet*
Knows what the other's saying!

257

Baseball 3256

*T*he archeologists
They dug
Some hundreds of years later
In a place they
Called the Bronx
In some gigantic crater

What was this coliseum?
Did Tigers come to roar?
They say, that they
Just might find one
From 1964

But left are only remnants
Of empty beer can cases
And spots of grass
And broken seats
And white bags they called, "bases"

And then they found one
In the Bronx
Called Yankel's Stadium
They figured millions
Had been there
But did not know "How come?"

"Why did so many
People flock
To that gigantic park?"
"Why did the millions
Roar and scream
Hours after dark?"

In just one year, two massive stadiums were built in New York. Bashevkin wonders what archeologists will say when they dig through the ruins of these mammoth coliseums and find out that all that happened there was men hitting balls with sticks.

Men would come
Each holding sticks
Their hands
Covered in leather
Around they'd run
In sweltering sun
(But not in rainy weather)

They found a high pile
Of brown dirt
Like two feet off the ground
"A King," they said
"Would stand on it"
They once called it
"The Mound"

"And as the King ascended
The simple folks
They cheered
And in his hand
He held something
That every
Stick man feared

"It was some magical
White orb
Which sunk and sped
And swerved
And sometimes slid
And sometimes changed
And very often curved

"And directly
In front of him
A masked man crouched
    quite low
And gestured to the
King on high
Which way, the orb to throw

The archeologists
Knew not
Where all stick men
Would roam
And why they seemed to
Run at first
And then try
To come back home

It seems the king
He hurled an orb
At some fantastic speed
The men at home
Would swing their sticks
And try to intercede

And as the orb
Came speeding by
They all would try their hacks
These costumed men
With funny names
And numbers
On their backs

We found some scratches
In the dirt
Where all the stickmen slid
Why not just walk?
We all did balk
Why run the way they did?

"They used to keep
Some oxen here"
The sign, it reads "Bull Pen"
I think the king he lost control
And then, we think is when

They called a bull
To come and gore
The beat up, hounded king
Who stood upon
His royal mound
As they hit everything

What silly customs
These men had
A stick, an orb, a team
And why would subjects
Sit high up
To spend a night and scream?

And then ...

A scientist came running
"We found not one, but two!
Why would New York
Need two such fields
One certainly would do!"

We'll never figure out their way
What a waste and what a pity
If they had a place for "Yankel"
Why make a place called "Citi"

In Lieu for You!

*T*his year's *Mishloach Manos*
I don't know what to do
So I guess I'll stop my worries
And just send, an 'in lieu'!

"In lieu of *mishloach manos*
I'm sending you this note
And in your honor, I have sent
A check to three mosdot!

"We're sorry we're not sending
No chocolate or fine wine
'Cause this year I have sent a check
To a *tzedakah* of mine"

I thought that's really interesting
In fact I thought it cool
Imagine if I could do that
For every single rule

I won't look for an *esrog*
'Cause that is often hard
I will just send the merchant
A brightly colored card

"I'm not buying an *esrog*
No need to look for flecks
Instead I'll send some *mosdos*
A couple of nice checks"

I know that Mishloach Manos can get costly and cumbersome, but the proliferation of sending "mitzvah notes" as a substitution makes Bashevkin ponder. After all, so many other mitzvos and activities are expensive as well. Why not just send notes for them, too?

261

I need not set menorahs
I need not twist a wick
I'll send a card
That's not too hard
And it can do the trick

It may even work for weddings
A new response card kind
We won't reserve a seat for you
I'm sure you will not mind!

Don't need to send a gift back
Or say if you'll attend
Instead just choose a charity
To them a gift you'll send

No more crunching *matzoh*
Or blowing *shofar* too
'Cause you can send a card
that says
"I'm doing this in lieu!"

Why not take it further
Now here's a real nice test
Where "in lieu" would really work
Where some would like it best

In lieu of a new Lexus
I bought a beat up Ford
And sent a card with a big check
To a *mosad* I've adored

Imagine if at weddings
No flowers would they place
"In lieu of flowers we
have helped
A real *rachmanus* case!"

And then a strange thing
happened
I think it was in July
I got *mishloach manos*
From someone who stopped b

Inside the simple basket
A crumpled note I saw
Inside the box with *hamantash*
They left beside my door

"The money that I owe you
I cannot really pay
But here's *mishloach manos*
For that's my way to say

"In lieu of paying up my debt
Which I felt was too hard
I sent *mishloach manos*
With this brightly colored carc

I mean not to knock *tzedaka*
Or brightly colored notes
But let's not substitute *mitzvos*
With types of antidotes!

The Next Text

The tapping was fast
Like the beat of the drums
But it wasn't of sticks
'Twas the tapping of thumbs

The thumbs worked hard
The thumbs worked fast
They had to get
The message passed

Click, click, type
Tap, tap, send
Will the texting
Ever end?

Past the teacher
Past the mom
From the Blackberry®
To the Palm®

Eyes are glued
To the tiny screen
Always downcast
Never seen

And in an instant
Lightning speed
Words appeared
For him to read

Texting has become so common that it has become a verb that is conjugated. Kids no longer speak even when they sit next to each other, instead they tap messages.

No more talking
No more speech
When your friend
You want to reach

Urgent, pressing
Message sent
This is how
The wording went

"What's up friend
How's it going?"
Followed by
A smile showing ☺

How important!

Such a text
Waiting for
The reply, next

With the flick
Of the thumb
'Twas back
On its way
The vital reply
Just read "OK"

The newfound type
Of communication
That suddenly
Has swept our nation

Worlds away?
Traversing miles
To send the texts
The frowns ☹, the smiles ☺

And so the message
Reached the friend
A vital question
He did send

However one day
He will ponder
When his age
Is way down yonder

Why did he have to
Text to me?
When he was sitting
Next to me?

Cars For Who?

I sat inside my car last week
Again I was frustrated
The light, it glared, "an oil leak"
Of course, anticipated

So I pulled in
To have it fixed
Truly considered junking
Enough repairs
And no AC
And cars behind me
Honking

But then the radio
(which worked)
Blared out some great news
Donate your car to charity
And help your fellow Jews

Five charities
All want my car
I can't imagine why
They offered a vacation
And two tickets to fly

What's the catch?
Are they for real?
Why would they want
My car?
The AC's broke
The oil leaks
It won't go very far

265

Then I heard the secret
I thought I lost my mind
The car is to be given
To people who are blind

Why Heritage would
Let them drive
I really had no clue
But if the blind
Would need a car
I guess that mine would do

In just a few more minutes
Commercial two of five
This time they said
The "Kars For Kids"
That were too young to drive!

Just then I passed a billboard
And I was not amused
There was a kid inside a car
I simply was confused!

Kids wouldn't mind my clunker
With dents on every side
They surely never had a car before
For they're too young to ride

The radio then blared some news
Then an ad came on once more
The ones who wanted cars this time
Made me hit the floor

I guess it was a place
That taught Sobriety
But I'd be scared
To give a car
To a L'Chaim Society!

I'm not sure
Where my car would go
If that's where I donated
But in my books
"L'Chayim's" said
when one's intoxicated!

Of course
I talk
With tongue in cheek
For this is just a musing

I'm sure
That it's a mitzvah
If your car
You plan on losing

The blind they are not drivin
Not drunks, and not a kid
So if you got a klunker
Why not help a fellow *Yid*?

Much Ado About Nothing

Nothing
Is a word
That is most absurd
It's much too often
Said and heard
When clearer thoughts
Would be preferred

Used as much as
"Everything,"
"Nothing" has
A special ring

When something you
Don't want to say
You hope that they
Will go away

Used all the time
They fight and shout
And then you ask,
"What's that about?"

"Nothing . . . "

It's what you have
You're sick in bed
They ask you what
The doctor said

"Nothing . . . "

They seem to take you
For a fool
You ask them what
They learned in school

"Nothing . . . "

He called you in
The other day
"What did your
Mean boss
Really say?"

"Nothing . . . "

What did you think
Of that piece of art?
When asked by
Someone very smart

"Nothing . . . "

"Your principal left
A message
On the phone
Why was there
Frustration noted
In his tone?"

"Nothing . . . "

The word "nothing" is often used by our teenage children to describe just about ... everything!

The child whimpers
Looks so grim
And, so you ask
What's bothering him

"Nothing . . . "

The wedding's really
Almost here
And do you know
What I have to wear?

"Nothing . . . "

The restaurant where
You went to eat
Whadja have?
What kind of treat?

"Nothing . . . "

He talked and talked
'Bout half the day
What did
The politician say?

"Nothing . . . "

I wonder why
A word so used
Is meaningless
And much abused

In fact, it leaves me
Quite confused
Indeed the word
Is so misused

And so my friend
These words I string
This poem I pen
This song I sing

Says "Nothing's" really

        . . . "Everything"

Take a Seat

You think that life
Is getting hard
Try to make
A seating card

With uncles, aunts
Avos, bonim
And your father's
Mechutanim

Near the band
Near the door
Who will sit on
The dance floor

If the hall
Was only bigger
My wife wouldn't sit
Near the *shvigger*

The band's too loud
I can't sit there
Try Uncle Moishy
He cannot hear

Near the door
Is way too cold
Gimple's Ninety-Six
Years old

Do they have
For handicap?
A place for
Yingelach to nap?

I really do not
Want my back
To face the big
Mechitzah crack

Will he like
With whom he's sitting
Or am I two
Disputers pitting

Do I know
Each one's *gesheft*
Who will be the
Last one left

Will one want
To say a *vort*
Next to one
Who'd just cavort?

Why do I worry?
Why do I care?
The whole thing is a
One night affair!

And my guests
I think should share
The fact that they
Are coming here

To make my *simcha*
So complete
So why do they care
How I seat?

269

Musing Memorials

Torah, Torah Chigri Sak

*T*orah, Torah
Chigri sak
A sea of tears
Block after block

Tear-streaked faces
Told the tale
Transcended age
That doleful wail

That cry did reach
The world afar
Way past Ocean
Way past "R"

The holy Mir
Was left to part
With Torah's *lev*
Its pulsing heart

Across the globe
The cry has grown
A broken crown
An empty throne

The orphans' cries
A child's love
Pleading to
The One Above

Who will lead
A Torah world?
Where every word
From him unfurled
Declared the glory
Of Your word
Nothing else
Was said or heard

The Torah took
A human form
Its might unleashed
A raging storm
And yet so gentle
Yet so warm

A Torah with
Human *levush*
Epitomizing
Lo Yomush

A fire raging
An earthquake's shatter
Yet comfort for
The smallest matter

Of a Talmid's
Every need
To grow
To *shteig*
To just succeed

The passing of a Rosh Yeshiva is compared to the destruction of the Bais HaMikdash. In the petirah of Mirrer Rosh Yeshiva, Rav Shmuel Birnbaum zt"l, every one of the thousands who attended the levaya saw the tears of the Sifrei Torah as they moistened the walls of that great citadel of Torah, Mirrer Yeshiva.

And that zest
That endless zeal
A *patish* strength
Of Torah steel

Breaking rocks
In countless pieces
A *ma'ayan hamisgaber*
The flow increases

And where he went
And where he'd go
The only thing
He'd want to know
Not "*Vos hertzach*"
Not "*Vos iz neias*"

It meant just nothing
In his eyes
The only care
The one concern
"How did
the *Tosafos*, the *Rashba* learn?"

The sweetest sound
All that he heard
Hurivin
On *Tosafos'* word

And now that symbol
That *demus*
Of Torah's essence
Its *mahus*

Has left this
Earthly plain domain
To the place
Of *Emes* reign

And hundreds cried
And thousands wailed
The *aron kodesh*
Bare, unveiled

The world of Torah
A great tear
Dripping down
The face of Mir

And from the wooden
Walls inside
The *Sifrei Torah*
Joined and cried

Yes!
The *Aron Kodesh*
Saw ascend
A cherished soul
Their dearest friend

All *Sifrei Torah*
Cried today
A Living Torah's
Gone away

Yehi zichro boruch.

We Are Mumbai

*H*ow does one manage
Not to cry
As he ponders
Wonders, "Why?"
He chose them
Not "Me," not "I"
To write the saga
Of Mumbai

What's there to write?
What's there to say?
About a morbid
Dreadful day
A day of carnage
In Bombay
Brought to our homes
From far away

A world so distant
So far-flung
The banner of Hashem
Was hung
A song of comfort
Was once sung
And now it mourns
Its martyred young

Whoever went
Would always feel
The Holtzberg's warmth
A place, a meal

An oasis of *Yiddishkeit*
In a foreign land
Where Jews all came
As different folks
And left as one
to band

Where *golus* took
A tiny break
An Indian respite
Where somehow
Diverse worlds
Would meet
Yet, everyone would fit

But terror's sword
Reached far and wide
And found us
'Round the world
Yishmael's flag
It would not hide
Its filthy wrath unfurled

A tearful lesson
To us did teach
A thought
We all must know
Until we
Correct the breach
There's no place they
won't go

The murder of the kedoshim at the Chabad House in Mumbai was a knife in the heart of our people. Yet it bound us so strongly reminding us that our souls are but from One Source and they shall unite there, once more.

275

To run. to hide
We all can try
But where we are
Is still Mumbai

Not comforts
in a Boro Park
Nor fancy homes
In Sutton Park
Can keep the light
From turning dark

A bustling metropolis
Where the Torah's
Words do reign
A tiny, lonely *shtetel*
Somewhere in the Ukraine

Are no safer than
The Chabad House
Where *Yidden*
Came to pray

The two who did transform it
from the House of Nariman
To a House of Jewish love
A model, paragon

To find a breath
Of *ruchniyus*
In the smog of
Old Bombay

A hotel
In Netanya
Or a bus in
Tel Aviv
A rural street
In Iowa
Where *Yidden*
Hardly live

There's *golus* in Bnei Brak
And hatred
On the wall
Skinheads in Toronto
And bombs in Montreal

There's always a reminder
That nowhere
Are we free
And that there is
No "type" of *Yid*
For every "them" is me

No matter where
We're standing
What street we're on
The lessons are eternal
Of a House called Nariman

No matter where we travel
No matter where we fly
Golus seems to find us
For everywhere's Mumbai

There are no sects in *golus*
And no rift does exist
For we are "one"
To all of "them"
To every terrorist

But if everywhere is *golus*
And all Jews are just one
Perhaps there is *nechama*
In the mayhem that was done

We were all shot together
We limp as we are maimed
The dreadful storm we'll weather
With each bullet that they aimed

We're Toldos Avram Yitzchak
Chabad and Bobov, too
We are Israeli tourists
And a Mexicana Jew

Maybe we are still standing
Indeed we're still alive
But maybe we are Moishele
The baby who'd survive

For *Klal Yisroel's yasom*
Whose tears wet every heart
Is the symbol of our history
A message to impart

That no matter how they'll kill us
Whatever time or where
Moishele will yet live on
A hope for our despair

Amongst the smoke and rubble
Like a baby 'mongst the reeds
A plant amidst the trouble
The Almighty always seeds

Until *Moshiach's* heralding
When all the dead revive
The Moisheles declare our fate
"*Klal Yisroel* will survive!"

Ode to My Two Bunkmates

A few years ago, two friends from decades back, Mitch Merlis and Yussie Shneider, ob"m passed away. Back then it was a different time, when dress and appearances did not matter much. People were judged by the content of their character. And though these two very special people were from different backgrounds and diverged on different paths, each serving Hashem in his own way. They each left an indelible mark on so many hundreds of people. Bashevkin, though called by a different name back then, is proud to have called himself a friend to the end.

I lost two friends this year
I haven't seen for ages
But the story of those men and times
I tell you through these pages

They were so different
Both of them
And, different, so was I
But the closeness of
Our differences
Is that, what makes me cry
For thirty years
Since my camp days
A different time and place

But when we met
Some decades down
We held in an embrace

But now they're gone
Each one so young
Just leaving memories
Of summers spent
In a special place
On the shores of Chodekee

One boy's name was Yussie
The other one was Mitch
We spent summer together
In a place that filled a niche

Our bunk was quite a mixture
Of Jews from
'Round the world
Some had long hair
Some had crew cuts
Some *payos* that were curled

Willigers, Wisilskis
A Kamenetzky too
We had a Brucee and a Jacky
In that summer's motley crew

Brucee had an outside shot
That never missed its place
And Nachman couldn't hit a lick
He never reached first base

Yet, after all was said and done
One kid shone like a star
His name was Yussie Schneider
The sweetest kid by far
Quite good on the playing field
Perhaps not the best
But no one could
Come near to him
On a *Mishnayos* test

And then there was another kid
He could shoot and hit and pitch
The strongest of the group by far
His name, he said, was "Mitch"

And Mitch he was a *gibor*
He'd smack the winning run
While Yus' would win
the Torah Bowl
Always second to none

So when someone
Struck out swinging
No one gave a spit
'Cause Mitch was in the order
And he'd surely get a hit

Such different kids
We were back then
Yet somehow it was fun
A summer of diversity
With *achdus* all as one

There was so much respect
The way we'd learn and play
What happened to that unity
That lived in Bunk *Chof-Hey*?

There was no word *yeshivish*
Each child was a boy
Who dressed the way his
Mom sent him
Dress or corduroy

We had Nickys and some Jackies
And Paul lay in the sun
But Jacky is now Yaakov
And Birnbaum is gone

While Nuti drew the banner
And "*Laiv* had reached the shore"
That shining summer season
Clearly shines no more

Yes, decades passed
And we moved on
We all went on our own
And Brucee is Rav Boruch
Some say he is a *gaon*

I met Yus' decades later
On some Manhattan street
And everything came back to us
Those years when all was sweet

We talked about the *chevrah*
The who, what, when and which
And then we wondered,
Both, aloud
"What happened to Mitch?"

Weeks later, I had heard the news
That *machlah* struck Mitch fast
The doctors gave him little hope
They said he would not last

But no, he would not let them
Say the things they said
He knew that God Almighty
Was standing in his stead

And for the weak and ailing
An ambassador so true
To spread only *emunah*
To every broken Jew

He cared not what
You wore to shul
Or what adorned your head
If you would need some *chizuk*
He's be there by your bed

Mitch crossed every boundary
An ambassador of *chizuk*
And pain embraced his once
Strong frame
With each step that he took

I saw Mitch in a hospital
The wounded giant, lame
He garnered all his strength
To hug
And call me by my name

He recalled that great era
Back in '64
When the only thing
that mattered
Was the spirit
. . . And the score

We laughed and cried a little
And he sent me on my way
No matter what the doctors said
I'm gonna walk one day
 And lo he found the power
To spread the words of strength
To help another human
He'd go to any length

And then that dreaded *machlah*
It next struck, one of us
It did not stop in Teaneck
It visited our Yus'

And Yus' he, too, would smile
Despite his severe pain
No matter who did wish him well
He said the same, *Amein*

He radiated sunshine
His faith shone from his face
With the smile of a summer time
From a different time and place

We lost a generation
Of people who were smart
Who looked beyond the clothing
To appreciate the heart
But I'm sure somewhere in Heaven
There is a Bunk *Chof-Hey*
Where Yussie learns *Mishnayos*
At least most of the day

And Mitch is his *chavrusah*
In that Diamond in the sky
As they wrestle through a *sugyah*
And we wrestle through the
"Why?"

Indeed they're bound together
Though different as could be

But that spirit, friend,
Did die and end

. . . On the shores of Chodekee

Born in Jamaica, Chester Robinson moved to Brooklyn at 12, dropped out of school at 16, became involved with drugs and worked for a hip-hop record label, and eventually ran his own company. But at age twenty-three, Chester left the life of crime and violence and rap to become Yoseph Robinson, a Ger Tzedek. He lectured on his achievements and his spiritual yearnings. In the summer of 2010, while working at a kosher wine and liquor store he was gunned down while protecting others in the store. Where as many in the rap business have taken bullets, as he did, Yoseph was killed with Shma on his lips while protecting others from harm.

Born on a small Island
Under Jamaica sun
Chester took a journey
That ended in a "One"

He came to these United States
And grew up in the "hood"
New York, Philly or LA
Never up to good

But soon a star for a dark world
He'd rock, he'd rant, he'd rap
With a smugness in his wicked smirk
Below his side-turned cap

And he'd point the crazy fingers
With scouts of "Hey!" and "Yo!"
And he'd "diss" you if you did not act
Like a young submissive bro'

The life of every party
With buddies, booze and drugs
And the only ones he called his friends
Were a vicious group of thugs

Around the land he'd travel
Spewing his strange rhyme
About his life of violence
And the cells where he spent time

But somewhere there was talent
And Chester he was able
To become a hip-hop star
And purchase his own "label"

A life like this would surely end
The way it did for his cronies
An overdose, a gunshot wound
And loads of tears from phonies

But my friend, to Robinson
A voice came to inspire
He opened up a *Chumash* and
He knew something was Higher

And slowly he climbed hurdles
And soon passed every test
He said, "When bad,
I was the worst,
As good, I'll be the best!"

Indeed "the best" he sought to be
He threw away his past
And everything he set to do
Would now forever last!

"My *tziztis* they inspire me
To resist my old lifestyle
And when I see those holy strings
My face breaks in a smile"

He left behind the hip hop
The drugs and rock and roll
Replaced by a
New, yearning Jew
With a pure and holy soul

His old friends
Saw him studying
Those thugs,
They jeered out loud
What is that old
Hirsch-Chumash book?
Come out with your old crowd!

But Chester was now Yoseph
Resisting every lure
He would not go back
To that sad life
That he had lived before

And then one day it happened
Hashem had made the call
His destiny, a Higher cause
Was how he'd have to fall

An evening in a liquor store
A robbery gone bad
"To save a life"
The only thought
That this *ger tzedek* had

He "took one" for another
R' Yoseph gave his blood
And on his lips
"Hashem is One"
Yatzoh nishmaso b'echad

His old friends
Many gone now
And he was shot like them

But, *Ashrecha*,
R' Yoseph
Nitfasta al kiddush Hashem

יוסף בן אברהם ע"ה

Glossary

H. Hebrew
Y. Yiddish
Ar. Aramaic

Achdus H. Unity

Adam le'ameil yulad H. "Man was born to toil" (Job 5:7)

Agudah H. lit. ref. to Agudath Israel

Ahavas Chinam H. Unconditional love (Ahava- Love Chinam - for nothing)

Aibishter Y. lit. most high. Refers to God

Aidel Y. Refined, well mannered

Aidim Y. Son-in-law

Ain Od Milvado H. No one but Him (God) (Deut. 4:35)

Ainikel (Ainiklach) Y. Grandchildren

Aishes Chayil H. Woman of Valor (Proverbs 32:1)

Al chait H. lit. "for the sin" (admission of guilt as part of repentance process of the Yom Kippur service)

Al pi darko H. lit. "According to his path", King Solomon's advice how to educate children (Proverbs 22:6)

Alef Bais H. First two letters of Hebrew alphabet (used as the Hebrew equivalent of ABCs)

Alter Yidden Y. Elderly Jews

Amain H. Amen

Ameilus H. Toil, esp. toiling in Torah learning

Anshei K'nesses Hagedolah H. Men of the Great Assembly

Arbah Minim H. Four Species (Lulav, Esrog, Hadassim, Aravos, used on Sukkos)

Arbeit macht unz frei Ger. "Work makes us free" slogan over Nazi concentration camps

Aron Kodesh H. Holy Ark containing Torah Scrolls

Atah Hareisah H. lit. "You taught" or directed (Deut. 4:35) Traditionally, its recital is sold on Simchas Torah

Av H. 1. father 2. Eleventh month in Jewish Calendar (see Tisha B'Av)

Avinu H. Our father

Avodah H. Work

Avos H. lit. Fathers (pl.) used as a nickname for Tractate Avos (Ethics of the Fathers)

Ayr mit tzveeble Y. Egg with onion (traditional Sabbath delicacy)

Badatz H. Acronym for "Beit Din Tzedek," or "Court of Justice," most often used to denote Jerusalem's High Court of the Chareidi community

Bais Hamikdash H. Holy Temple in Jerusalem

Bais Medrash Govoha H. Largest Yeshiva and Kollel in America (located in Lakewood, NJ)

Bais Yaakov H. lit. "House of Jacob," network of Orthodox girls' schools

Bais Yosef Commentary on Tur Shulchan Aruch by Rav Yosef Karo (1488-1575)

Bashert Y. Destined (refers to one's destined mate or destiny)

BaTorah, Klal Gadol H. Great rule in the Torah (Golden Rule)

Bayis Sheini H. 2nd Temple in Jerusalem

Bein hazmanim H. lit. Between sessions in Yeshiva

Ben H. son (of)

Benafsho yovi lachmo H. "With his soul he will bring bread" (make a living) from High Holy Day prayers

Bentsh (bentching) Y. To recite Grace after meals

Besurah H. Tidings

Bezei'as apecha H. "By the sweat of your brow" (Gen. 3:19)

Birah tochiach Ar. Hebrew expression, (Yoma 9b) The building will prove it., i.e. the lack of a Temple for close to 2000 years is proof that we have not mended our ways.

Bircas HaChamah H. Blessing recited in appreciation of the sun when it completes its cycle every 28 years

Bli ayin horah H. With no evil eye (usually follows a compliment)

B'nei Binah H. lit. The sons of the wise, wise men

Bnei Torah H. lit. Sons of Torah. those who follow Torah law and custom

Bochur(im) H. Unmarried man (men)

Boruch H. Blessed

Boruch Habah H. lit. Blessed are those who come, i.e. welcome

Bracha (Brachos) H. Blessing (s)

Bris (brissim) H. lit. Covenant, specifically circumcision

Brisk City in Eastern Europe where the Soloveitchik Dynasty began. 2. Yeshiva in Jerusalem founded by the Soleveitchik family

Bruck Y. Allowing Matzah to become wet on Passover (Chassidim refrain)

B'tailin Um'vutalin H. Completely nullified (from Kol Nidrei service)

B'yad Hashem *H.* In the hands of God
B'Yerushalayim habnuyah *H.* In rebuilt Jerusalem
Chabad Acronym for three levels of knowledge **Chochma, Binah, Da'as,** a reference to Lubavitch movement
Chaburah Group
Chachamim *H.* Wise men
Chai Lifeline Cancer support organization
Chairem *H.* Ban
Chapping *Yesh. lit.* catching (used for understanding)
Charoses *Ar.* Sweet, chunky paste of fruits and nuts eaten during the Passover Seder.
Chashuv *H.* Distinguished
Chassidim *H.* Hassidim
Chassidish *H.* Hassidic
Chaveirim *H. lit.* Friends, Jewish volunteer organization on the Eastern U.S. which assists people in emergencies
Chavrusa *Ar.* study partner
Chazal Sages (acronym of Chachameinu Zichronom L'vracha - Our sages, may their memory be a blessing)
Cheder (Chadorim) *lit.* room (refers to elementary Jewish school)
Cheirem *H.* Excommunication
Chesed (Chasodim) *H.* Kindness(es)
Chesbonon(os) *H.* Calculation(s)
Chevra (*Ar.*) Group
Chiddush *H.* Novel idea
Chodesh Kislev Month of Kislev (third month of year)
Choleh *H.* A sick person
Cholent Sabbath delicacy of meat, potatoes, barley, and beans
Chumash *H.* Bible
Churban *H.* Destruction (refers to destruction of Holy Temple)
Daf *H. lit.* page, short for Daf Yomi
Daf Yomi *H.* Daily regimen to study the Talmud one folio each day
Daled Kosos *H.* Four cups of wine drunk at Passover Seder
Darshening *Y.* Preaching
Daven/Davening *Y.* Pray
Dayeinu *H.* part of Seder liturgy
Demus *H.* Likeness
Derech Eretz *H.* Proper manners
Din *H.* Judgment
D'indarnoh See Kol Nidrei
Divrei mussar *H.* Ethical discourse

Dor *H.* Generation
Dov'vos *H.* Speaking
Dreidel *Y.* Toy top used on Chanukah
Dvar Torah (Divrei Torah) *H.* Torah thought
Eliyahu HaNavi *H.* Elijah the Prophet
Elul 12th month of the Jewish year
Emes *H.* Truth
Emunah *H.* Faith
Eretz Yisroel *H.* Land of Israel
Erev Pesach *H.* Day before Passover
Erev Yom Tov *H.* Day before Festival
Esah einai *H.* "I lift my eyes" (Psalms 121)
Esah el heharim *H.* Lift to the mountains (ibid)
Esrog *H.* Citron
Facht *Y.* a trade
Freier *Y. lit.* free, one who has shirked Torah observance
Frosk *Y.* smack
Gaavah *H.* Haughtiness
Gadol (Gedolim) *H.* Great man (men). Used to refer to Torah scholars
Gantz *Y.* Total
Gantzer tohg uhn nacht *Y.* All day and night
Gedolei Yisroel *H.* Great men of Israel
Geferlach *Y.* Terrible
Gelt *Y.* Money
Gemach Acronym for Gemilas Chessed (usually reference to a free loan fund)
Gemilus Chasadim *H.* Acts of kindness
Gemalasa tov V'lo Ra H. see Aishes Chayil
Gemara Talmud
Ger tzedek *H.* A righteous convert
Gesheft *Y.* Business
Geshmak *Y.* Delicious
Geulah *H.* Redemption
Gibor *H.* Strong man
Glaizel *Y.* Glass
Glick *Y.* Luck
Goilem *H.* Golem *lit.* form, dunce. Refers to the Golem made by Rabbi Yehuda Lowey of Prague
Golus *H.* Exile
Gornisht felt *Y.* Missing nothing
Groise *Y.* Huge
Groise nidge *Y.* A big bother or pain in the neck
Groise rachmanus *Y.* 1.Big pity (on him or her), 2. one who is pitifully unlucky
G'vir (g'virim) *H.* Wealthy person(s)

Habah lehargecha hashkeim l'hargo *H.* "One who arises to kill you, kill him first" (Talmud)

HaBayta *H.* Homeward bound

Hadasim *H.* Myrtle used in four species

Hadar *H.* Beauty

Hagados Pl. of Haggadah. Book of Passover Seder service and protocol

Hallel *H.* Psalms said during prayer on Rosh Chodesh and Holidays

HaMakom *H. lit.* The place, refers to God

Hamantash *Y.* Triangle shaped Purim pastry

Har *H.* Mount, Mountain

Hartz *Y.* Heart, feel

Hashem *H.* God

Hashem echad *H.* God is One

Hasogas g'vul *H. lit.* "encroaching borders" i.e. unfair business competition

Hatzolah A Volunteer ambulance corp.

Heartzik *Y.* Hearty, warm

Hee she'Amda *H.* "This stood for us" (part of the Passover Seder)

Heichal *H.* Part of the Bais HaMikdash

Heilige *Y.* Holy

Heimish *Y. lit.* 1. At home with or comfortable with 2. Someone piously observant

Hisgabrus *H.* Overcoming something or oneself

Hock *Y.* v. Bother, disturb, n. Latest news, or gossip

Holech Tomim *H.* One who walks in righteousness (Psalms 15:2)

Hurivin *Y.* Toil in Torah study

I'lmalei mora'ah *Ar.* "if not for fear" (of the government) (Avos 3:2)

Ir HaTorah *H.* City of Torah

Ish l'reiyeihu *H.* Each man to his friend

Iyar, Eighth month in Jewish calendar

kabalos *H.* Resolution accepted on oneself

Kain ayin hara *H. lit.* With no evil eye (intended) Same as bli ayin hara

Kanfei Nesharim *H.* On eagles' wings (Exodus 19:4)

Kapara *H.* Atonement

Kasha (s) *Y.* Question(s)

Kavod *H.* Honor, Respect

Kavod lo nahagu *H.* They didn't show respect

Kedoshim *H.* 1. Holy ones 2. Martyrs

Kehuna *H.* Priesthood

Keili lama azavtani *H.* "My God, why

have You forsaken me" (Psalms 22)

Keren HaShmittah *H.* Organization which helps farmers who observe the Sabbatical year

Keshaashuay Be'onyee *H.* "Like my comfort in my distress" (Psalms 119:92)

Kever Ruchel Imeinu (Imeinee) *H.* Rachel's tomb

Kesher *H.* A tie, connection

Ki lekach tov nosati *H.* "Because goodness I given you" (Proverbs 4:2)

Kibud Av V'aim *H.* Honoring parents

Kinderlach *Y.* Children

Kineged Zachor V'Shamor *H.* Remembering and guarding (Sabbath)

Kinyan Torah *H.* Acquiring Torah

Kippah S'rugah *H.* Crocheted yarmulka

Kisei HaKavod *H.* God's throne of glory

Kislev Third month of Jewish Calendar

Kisvei Chofetz Chaim *H.* Writings of Chofetz Chaim (R. Yisroel Meir Kagan 1837-1933)

Kiyum *H.* Existence

Klal Yisroel *H.* The Jewish people

Kler *Y.* 1. v. to debate two sides n. a question with varying aspects

Klopping, klopped *Y.* Striking, struck

K'nock *Y.* Knock

Kochos *H.* Strength

Kol Koreh *H.* Announcement (usually printed)

Kol Nidrei Inaugural Yom Kippur service releasing all vows.

Kollel (kollelim) *H.* Framework where married men learn Torah

Kool'hone Icharatna B'hon *Ar.* Part of Kol Nidrei

Kool'hone y'hon Shoron *Ar.* Part of Kol Nidrei

Korbanos *H.* Sacrifices

Kos *H.* Cup

Kosel (Kosel Ma'arovi) *H.* Western Wall

K'tores *H.* Incense

K'tzos Commentary on Shulchan Aruch (R. Aryeh Leib Hacohen Heller) (1745-1812)

Kugel *Y.* Sabbath delicacy of noodles, potatoes, or other vegetables

Kuntz *Y.* n. A trick

Kupas HaIr *H.* Charity fund in Israel

Kutzo shel Yud *H.* The point of the Hebrew letter Yud, essential for validity of Tefillin, Mezuzos and Torah scrolls

Kvell *Y.* To glow with pride

Kvetch *Y.* To complain

Kvetch the benk *Y.* Sit on a bench reference (often derogatory) to those who sit all day studying Torah

Laiv Melachim V'sarim *H.* "The heart of kings and princes…"

Lashon Horah *H.* Evil speech, gossip

Lashon ilgim *H.* Poor language, cockney (tongue of the stammerers, Isaiah 32:4)

L'chaim *H.* To life! (a toast)

Lekach tov *H.* Good advice

Levush Compendium of Jewish law by Mordecai ben Avraham Yoffe , 1600's 2. *H.* garment,

Licht (lichtilach) *Y.* Light (s)

Limud Torah *H.* Learning Torah

Lo Shririn V'Lo Kayamin *Ar. see Kol Nidrei*

Lo yomush *H.* Will not wither (Joshua 1:8)

L'shana HaBah B'Yerushalayim *H.* Next year in Jerusalem (Hagadah liturgy)

Luchos *H.* Tablets on which the 10 Commandments were written

Lulav *H.* Palm branch used on Sukkos

Ma'avir al midosuv *H.* Forgoing what one could demand

Ma'ayan misgaber *H.* Never ending fountain (Avos 2:12)

Machanayim *H.* Game similar to dodgeball

Macher *Y.* A "shaker and maker"

Machlah *H.* Illness, esp. cancer

Machzik *H. v.* Support

Machzor *H.* Holiday prayer book

Magid Shiur *H.* Torah lecturer

Mahus *H.* Identity

Maidel *Y.* Girl

Makom Mikdash *H.* Place of the Holy Temple in Jerusalem

Malach *H.* Angel

Malach HaMaves *H.* Angel of death

Malchus *H.* Royalty

Mar *H.* 1. Bitter 2. Mr.

Marcheshvan Second month of Jewish calendar

Maror *H.* Bitter herbs

Mashgiach *H. lit.* One who watches, refers to one who ensures that kashruth is being observed or a Dean of Ethics in a Yeshiva

Mashiv *H. lit.* Return, first word of the intonation begun Shmini Atzeres "Mashiv HaRuach Umorid HaGeshem (He who brings wind and lets rain)

Matana *H.* Gift

Mavucha *H.* Dilemma

Mazel *H.* Luck

Mechazek *H.* Strengthen, col. cheer up

Mechitzah *H. lit.* Separation, used as the separator between men and women in the synagogue

Mechutanim *H.* In-laws, the relation of parents or relatives of the bride to the parents and relatives of the groom

Mekor *H.* Source

Men tracht, Gut Lacht *Y.* We think, God laughs

Menachem avel *H.* To comfort a mourner

Meraglim *H.* Spies (refers to the spies of Biblical times)

Meshulach (meshulachim) *H. lit.* Those sent, usually fund raisers

Mesorah *H.* 1. n. Tradition 2. v. passed

Mevater *H.* Acquiesce

Mevushal *H.* Cooked

Middah *H.* An attribute, characteristic

Mikva (Mikvaos) *H.* Ritualarium

Minnim *H.* 1. Types 2. heretics

Minyan (Minyanim) *H.* Quorum of 10 men

Mir Town in Poland. 2. Yeshiva in Jerusalem and/ or Brooklyn, founded by survivors of the original Mir Yeshiva. Mirrer Yeshiva (Brooklyn) or (Yeshivas Mir) Jerusalem

Misaskim *H.* Volunteer organization that helps mourners

Mishebeirach *H.* "He who blessed" A prayer said on Shabbos

Mishloach manos *H.* Gifts of food sent on Purim

Mishnayos *H.* Sections of the Mishnah

Misnagdim *H. lit.* Those who are against non-Chassidim

Mizrach *H.* East

Mocher Seforim *H.* Jewish book seller

Monn *H.* Manna

Morah (Moros) *H.* Teacher(s)

Mosad (mosdot, mosdos) *H.* Institution

Moshe *H.* Moses

Moshiach *H.* The Messiah

Mussar (mussar shmuess(en)) *H. lit.* Ethical discourse(s)

Na'aseh V'Nishmah *H.* "We will do and we will hear" (Exodus 24:7)

Nachamu, nachamu (ami) *H.* "Comfort, comfort (my people)" (Isaiah 40:1)

Nahafoch hu *H.* "And it will be turned around" (Esther 9:1)

Nairos *H.* Candles

Navi (nevi'im) *H.* Prophet(s)

Navi Yirmiyahu *H.* Jeremiah the Prophet

Nebby *Y.* nebbish *see* groiseh rachmanus

Nechama *H.* Consolation

Negel vasser *Y.* Water for washing hands in the morning

Neis *H.* Miracle

Ner (ref. to Ner Yisroel) *H. lit.* light. Many Yeshivos contain the word Ner as a prefix

Neshama *H.* Soul

Nesivos Commentary on Shulchan Aruch CM by Rav Yaakov Loberbaum of Lissa (1760-1832)

Nidrana Lo Nidrei *Ar.* see Kol Nidrei

Niggun (niggunim) *H.* Spiritual tune(s),

Nisayon *H.* Spiritual test

Nissan Sixth month of the Jewish calendar

Ohr *H.* Light

Ohr haganuz *H.* The hidden light

Ohz *H.* Strength

Olam (Oilam) *H.* World

Ois'geklunked *Y. Ois* Out with (the Klunker Program). Ois in Yiddish is a reference to "Out with" geklunked, a feference to klunker cars. (A Bashevkin portmanteau)

Oretz *H.* Earth

Oro shel Livyasan *H.* Hide of the leviathan

Os *H.* 1.Sign 2. Letter in Heb. alphabet

Osei ma'aseh Bereishis *H. lit.* The One who caused the creation (blessing made on miraculous wonders of creation)

Oz yimalei *H.* "Then shall be filled (our mouths with laughter) ref. to Messianic era (Psalms 126:2)

P'shat *H.* Simple meaning of the text

Pakod Pakad'tee *H.* "I shall surely remember" (Exodus)

Parnassah *H.* Livelihood

Pas *H.* Bread

Patish *H.* Hammer

Payos *H.* Sidelocks

Pekalach *Y.* Small packages, esp. of treats or troubles

Pesach *H.* Passover

Pesach Sheini *H.* Second Passover held a month after the usual Passover

Pgisha *H.* Meeting

Pittim *H.* Uppermost and most fragile part of esrog

Pizmonim *H.* Liturgical ballads (usually composed by Medieval Sages)

Ponim *H.* Face

Poshut *H.* Simple

Psak *H.* Final ruling in a case

Rabbim *H.* Many

Rabbosai *Ar.* Gentlemen

Rachmana Litzlan *Ar.* May God save us

Rakeves *H.* Train

Rashba Commentator on Talmud (Rabbi Shlomo ben Aderes (1235–1310)

Rebbi (rabbeim) Rabbi, sometimes teacher

Redt *Y.* Suggest a match

Rivka B'suel's Rebecca, daughter of Besuel

Rivka Imeinu Rebecca, (*lit.* our mother) the Matriarch

Rosh Yeshiva *H.* Dean of Yeshiva

Roshei Sanhedrin *H.* Heads of the ancient Supreme Court

R'tzai *H.* Addition to grace after meals on the Sabbath

Ruchnius *H.* Spirituality

Sar *H.* Prince

Sar HaMashkim *H.* Steward of drinks in Egypt

S'chach *H.* Covering for a Sukkah

Sechorah *H.* 1.Merchandise 2. Buisness

Seder (sedarim) *H. lit.* Order 1. Passover Seder 2. Schedule of learning

Sefer (seforim) *H.* Book(s) of Torah literature

Sefirah *H.* Counting of the omer

Segulah (segulos) *H.* Custom or acts based on Talmudic, Kabbala or tradition, meant to aid in attaining specific goals

Seudah *H.* Meal

Seudah Shlishis *H.* Third meal on the Sabbath

Shaarei Teshuva *H. lit.* Gates of Repentance title of Book by Rabbein Yona of Gerondi (died 1263) outlining the path to proper penitence

Shabbos *H.* Sabbath

Shadchan *H.* Matchmaker

Shaifeleh *Y.* Dear

Shailah *H.* Question

Shaitel *Y.* Wig

Shaitel macher Y. Wig stylist
Shamayim H. Heaven
Shandeh Y. Shame, scandal
Shayur H. see shiur
Shedra H. Spine
Shemesh H. Sun
Shevarim H. 1. lit. Broken pieces 2. A
 sound of the shofar (3 short blasts)
Shiur (Shiurim) H. 1. Torah Class
 2. measurement
Shiva home H. House of mourners
Shlep Y. 1. Pull something along 2.
 Exert self to go somewhere
Shliach H. Messenger
Shlit"a H. Acronym for may he live
 good and long days
Shmeichel Y. Smile
Shmiras HaLoshon H. Guarding one's
 tongue from gossip
Shmoozing/Shmooz Y. 1. Casual talk 2.
 ethical discourse
Shmos H. Book of Exodus
Shmurah H. Guarded ref. to Matzah
 process that is carefully watched
 from time of harvest to ensure it does
 not leaven
Shnorrer Y. Beggar
Shomrim H. lit. Watchmen 2. Volunteer
 organization that aids the Police
Shpiel Y. 1. Pitch (as in fundraising or
 politics) 2. play (as on stage)
Shprach Y. Language
Shtender Y. Lecturn
Shtetl Belz Y. Town of Belz in Galicia
Shtick Y. Funny tricks and such
Shtuch Y. Poke (fun)
Shtup(ped) Y. Stuff(ed) something into
Shuckled Y. Swayed
Shul Y. Synagogue
Shveig Y. To keep quiet
Shver Y. Father in law
Shvigger Y. Mother in law
Shvikin…. Shvisin Ar. see Kol Nidrei
Shvitz(ed) Y. 1. Sweat(ed)
Siddur H. Prayer book
Sifrei Mussar H. Books of Jewish ethics
Sifrei Torah H. Torah scrolls
Simcha (Simchos) H. Happy
 occasion(s)
Sinas Chinam H. Baseless hatred
Siyata DiShmaya Ar. Heavenly help
Siyum H. Celebration made upon
 completion of a tractate of Gemarah
 or Mishne

Slicha (Slichos) H. Penitential prayers
Sonim H. Adversaries
Stam H. Vanilla, plain, generic
stirah Contradiction
Sugya Ar. Portion of Talmud
Sukkah (sukkos) H. Tabernacle
Sukkas Dovid H. Holy Temple in
 Jerusalem
Sukkele Y. Little Sukkah (endearment)
S'vorah Ar. Logic
Tallis H. Prayer shawl
Talmid (talmidim) H. Student(s)
Talmid Chochom (Talmidei
 Chachomim) H. Torah scholar(s)
Tanaim H. Sages of the Mishnah
Tayna Ar. Complaint
tchotchkes Y. Knickknacks
Techias HaMeisim H. Revival of the
 dead
Teef Y. Deep
Tefillah (tefillos) H. Prayer
Tefillin Phylacteries
Tehillim H. Psalms
Teru'a (teru'os) H. Sound of the shofar
Teshuvah H. Repentance
Tichel Y. Head kerchief
Tikasayvu H. May we be inscribed
Tirutzim "feltnisht ois" Y. No lack of
 excuses
Tisha B'Av H. Fast of the ninth day of
 the Hebrew month of Av
Tishrei First month of the Jewish
 calendar
Tochacha H. Rebuke (portion in the
 Torah)
Tof H. Last letter of the Hebrew
 alphabet
Tomchei Shabbos H. Organization that
 provides food for Shabbos
Torah Lishmah H. Learning Torah
 without ulterior motives
Torah, Torah, chagri sak H. "Torah,
 Torah, don sackcloth"
Toras nigleh v'nistar H. Revealed and
 hidden Torah
Tosfos H. Compendium of medieval
 commentaries on the Talmud, mainly
 French
Toshvei Eretz Yisroel H. Inhabitants of
 the Land of Israel
Totty Y. Father
Tracht Y. Think(s)
Tumul Y. Commotion
Tzaddik H. Righteous person

Tzafun *H.* Hidden, esp. matza hidden at the Passover Seder

Tzedaka *H.* Charity

Tzipisah L'yeshuah *H.* Awaiting the redemption

Tzitzis *H.* Fringes worn on four cornered garment

Tzubrochen *Y.* Broken

U'diasarna al nafshasana *Ar.* see Kol Nidrei

U'Dishtabanoh *Ar.* see Kol Nidrei

U'fros (U'frosh aleinu) *H.* And spread (over us) Part of Maariv prayer.

Ugah belo hafucha *H.* An unturned cake. ie, half baked (Hosea 7:8)

U'nesaneh Tokef Part of High holiday prayer service

Ushpizin *Ar.* Heavenly guests in the Sukkah

U'shvuei *Ar.* see Kol Nidrei

U'shvusana, Lah Sh'vuos *Ar.* see Kol Nidrei

V'Charomay *Ar.* see Kol Nidrei

Vertlach *Y.* Words of Torah

V'esorei *Ar.* see Kol Nidrei

V'esrona Lo Esorei *Ar.* see Kol Nidrei

V'hee sheAmda *H.* "And this stood for us", part of Passover Seder

V'Kinusai, V'Chinuyai *Ar.* see Kol Nidrei

V'Konomai *Ar.* see Kol Nidrei

V'nomar amein! *H.* And let us say Amen

Vort *Y. lit.* Word of honor 2.Words (of Torah)

Vos eppes *Y.* What's going on?

Vos hertzach *Y.* What's is being heard?

Vos iz neis *Y.* What's new(s)?

Ya'aleh *H.* Let it Arise (ref. to Yaaleh V'yavoh a supplication added on Rosh Chodesh and festivals)

Yarmulka *Y.* Skullcap

Yehi zichro boruch *H.* May his memory be blessed

Yehoshua *H.* Joshua

Yemai Shemonah *H.* The eight days of Chanukah

Yemei HaRachamim *H.* The days of mercy

Yerushalayim *H.* Jerusalem

Yeshiva *H.* Torah school

Yeshiva Gedolah *H.* Higher school of Torah learning

Yeshua (yeshuos) *H.* Salvation

Yichus Lineage

Yid (Yidden) *Y.* Jew(s)

Yiddishe kinder *Y.* Jewish children

Yiddishkeit *Y.* Judaism

Yingle *Y.* Boy

Yom Acharon *H. lit.* The final day (Rashi. End of life) from Aishes Chayil (Proverbs 31:25)

Yom HaDin *H.* The day of judgment

Yom Shishi *H.* Friday

Yom Tov *H.* Festival

Yomim Nora'im *H.* The high holidays

Yosheiv in Himmel lacht *Y.* He who sits in heaven (God) laughs

Yungerman (Yungerleit) *Y. lit.* Young man (men) who learns Torah

Zaidy *Y.* Grandfather

Zaka Volunteer organization that deals with recovering and burying those killed in terrorist attacks or accidents

Zechus *H. n.* Merit

Z'kainim *H.* Elders

Zman Grama Time-bound Mitzvos

Zman Simchasainu *H. lit.* Time of our rejoicing, holiday of Sukkos

Zohar The foundational work of Jewish Kabbalah written by Rabbi Shimon Ben Yochai who lived in the era of the scholars of the Mishnah

Zoche *H. v.* Merit

In loving memory of...

our dear husband, father and grandfather

RABBI YITZCHOK AHRON SINGER זצ"ל

לעילוי נשמת ולזכר עולם

הרב יצחק אהרן בן הרב אליהו זללה"ה

נפטר י"ג טבת תשס"א

A רב for over four decades,
he inspired people from all walks of life
as a leader, teacher, and a מקרב לתורה.

Highly respected as a role model
for his greatness in תורה and as an inspiring דרשן
he was at the same time beloved for his warmth,
compassion and love for his fellow human being.

A scion of illustrious Rabbonim and Gaonim,
he perpetuated their legacy though his
תורה, עבודה, וגמילת חסדים.

יהא זכרו ברוך

Bluma Singer
Baruch and Susie Singer
Eli Hersh and Rivki Singer
Nussie and Ruchy Singer
Yossie and Suri Singer
Srulie Singer